From Tears to Triumph: Tales of Transformation through Jesus Christ

A Beauty From Ashes Anthology

Managing Editor, Alyssa Middleton

From Tears to Triumph: Tales of Transformation through Jesus Christ

Authors: Linda Bingham, Dr. Esly Carvalho, Katie Clifton, Elin Criswell, Andrea Crowder, Kayla Fioravanti, Julene Fleurmond, Vanessa Hlavaty, Dr. Lori Hobson, Mary Humphrey, Beverly Dru Lewis, Alyssa Middleton, Cheryl Moses, Loral Robben Pepoon, Patricia "Pat" Sabiston, Susan Sexton, Cindy Taylor, Alicia Terry, Amy Volk and Jennifer Waddle.

Managing Editor: Alyssa Middleton
Editor: Loral Robben Pepoon
Cover Design: Jennifer Smith

ISBN-13: 978-0692577769 (Beauty From Ashes Press)
ISBN:-10: 0692577769

Copyright © 2015 Beauty From Ashes Press
Printed in the United States of America
Published by Beauty From Ashes Press

Notice of Rights
All rights reserved. No part of this book may be reproduced or transmitted in any form by any means – electronic, mechanical, photocopy, recording or other – without the prior written permission of the publisher and/or the respective copyright owner. All articles submitted for publication in From Tears to Triumph are published under license from the author/copyright owner of such materials as noted below. Each other is responsible for the subject matter of the submitted material.

Disclaimer
All views and opinions expressed in From Tears to Triumph are solely those of the original author. The views and opinions do not necessarily represent those of Beauty from Ashes Press.

All Scripture quotations were verified by Bible Hub, Web. 9/26/2015. Used by permission. All rights reserved.

Copyright © 2014 Kayla Fioravanti: In the Arms of the Shepherd
Copyright © 2015 Linda Bingham: Vengeance is Mine Saith the Lord
Copyright © 2015 Dr Esly Carvalho: Counting My Blessings
Copyright © 2015 Katie Cifton: Draw Near, An Unlikely Friend
Copyright © 2015 Elin Criswell: Deceived No More
Copyright © 2015 Andrea Crowder: Multiple Miracles
Copyright © 2015 Julene Fleurmond: From Fear to Freedom: How Love Rescued Me
Copyright © 2015 Dr. Lori Hobson: The Prayer of Jabez Should Come with a Warning Label, And Let There Be Light!
Copyright © 2015 Vanessa Hlavaty: Cancer, God's Plan for Our Family
Copyright © 2015 Mary Humphrey: Dying to Self on Earth
Copyright © 2015 Beverly Dru Lewis: After the Wedding
Copyright © 2015 Alyssa Middleton: But for the Grace of God
Copyright © 2015 Cheryl Moses: Devastation from Domestic Violence Redeemed
Copyright © 2015 Loral Robben Pepoon: From Chicago Blues to Tennessee Bluebirds
Copyright © 2015 Patricia Sabiston: When God Calls, It's Never a Wrong Number
Copyright © 2015 Susan Sexton: Christopher
Copyright © 2015 Cindy Taylor: Letting God Reinvent My Purpose
Copyright © 2015 Alicia Terry: Identity Crisis
Copyright © 2015 Amy Volk: Living a Charade
Copyright © 2015 Jennifer Waddle: You Got Your Girl

Beauty For Ashes Press

DEDICATION

To D.M., the first woman I met who proudly declared her brokenness and subsequent redemption in Christ, whose joy of salvation and victorious living was utterly infectious.

Your unwavering enthusiasm for the Lord and His Word has touched and stayed with me for decades. I am blessed to have been part of your life for a season.

CONTENTS

DEFEATING ABUSE AND DOMESTIC VIOLENCE

1	But for the Grace of God by Alyssa Middleton	1
2	Devastation from Domestic Violence Redeemed by Cheryl Moses	9
3	In the Arms of the Shepherd by Kayla Fioravanti	19

EMBRACING EXTRAORDINARY CALLINGS

4	And Let There Be Light! By Dr. Lori M. Hobson	31
5	Counting My Blessings by Dr. Esly Carvalho	35
6	Dying to Self on Earth by Mary Humphrey	41
7	From Fear to Freedom: How Love Rescued Me by Julene Fleurmond	45
8	Letting God Reinvent My Purpose by Cindy Taylor	51
9	When God Calls, It's Never a Wrong Number by Pat Sabiston	59

LISTENING TO GOD'S LIFE-GIVING WORDS

10	Deceived No More by Elin Criswell	69
11	Draw Near by Katie Clifton	75
12	From Chicago Blues to Tennessee Bluebirds by Loral Robben Pepoon	81
13	Identity Crisis by Alicia Terry	93

MOVING MOUNTAINS IN MARRIAGE

| 14 | After the Wedding by Beverly Dru Lewis | 101 |
| 15 | I Am a Sinner of the Worst Kind by Anonymous | 107 |

PERSEVERING WITH UNIMAGINABLE PEACE

16	Cancer by Vanessa Hlavaty	113
17	Christopher by Susan Sexton	115
18	Vengeance is Mine Saith the Lord by Linda Bingham	125
19	You Got Your Girl by Jennifer Waddle	131

PRAYING POWERFUL PRAYERS

20	God's Plan for Our Family by Vanessa Hlavaty	137
21	The Prayer of Jabez Should Come with a Warning Label by Dr. Lori M. Hobson	141
22	An Unlikely Friend by Katie Clifton	145

RECEIVING REMARKABLE REDEMPTION

23	Living a Charade by Amy Volk	151
24	Multiple Miracles by Andrea Crowder	155
	ABOUT THE AUTHORS	165
	ACKNOWLEDGEMENTS	177

DEFEATING ABUSE AND DOMESTIC VIOLENCE

BUT FOR THE GRACE OF GOD
By Alyssa Middleton

When I look back at the path that I was once on, and where that path would have led if I had stayed, I shudder in disbelief. My current life is so different from what it was 12 years ago. It is truly because of God's grace that I am able to share my story today.

I was raised in a strict, controlling Christian family, and like many raised that way, I rebelled. I was constantly pushing the limits as I grew and chafed against the religious requirements of attending church each Wednesday and Sunday and spending hours in Confirmation classes. I don't recall hearing much about God's grace and compassion other than on Easter Sunday. Instead, my perception of God was that of a strict and supreme ruler, always watching and waiting for me to mess up. There was an unattainable level of perfection that He required. Even after confessing my sins, I still felt like I had to atone more. I thought that simply asking for forgiveness wasn't enough.

I desperately longed for attention and approval. I wanted to live in a place where I was appreciated for being me, and I didn't want to have to face rejection—or the threat of not being good enough. When I was 14, I discovered that promiscuity brought me male attention that I'd been yearning for. For years, I experienced short bursts of affection and belonging as I cycled through boyfriend after boyfriend. The unconditional love I sought was elusive. Although these "relationships" fizzled quickly, there was always another guy "in the wings," as my reputation for being "easy" preceded me.

It was only by the grace of God that I never ended up pregnant or contracting a sexually transmitted disease. I was young—far too young and naïve—and I gave no thought to future consequences.

Off I went to college, where I simply focused on having fun and celebrating the freedom that came from moving out of my parent's house at 17. The days of strict control were behind me, and I experimented with drinking and drugs. I was attempting to fill an ever-present loneliness and desire to belong and be accepted. Of course, sex, drugs and rock and roll never satisfy a space that only God can fill.

In graduate school, I made a choice that changed the trajectory of my life forever. I was dating a known alcoholic and drug abuser, with a history of criminal offenses dating back to when he was a juvenile. I didn't drink nearly as often, nor do many drugs at that point because I was in school full time, earning my master's degree and also working to pay for school. But, I did let this smooth-talking hustler fill my ears with praise and lies. We shared a connection of feeling like outsiders. It seemed like the world was against us, but that we could save each other from sinking. He quickly moved into my apartment and we became increasingly and unhealthily dependent upon each other as my circle of support shrank (something I saw after the fact as a normal part of the cycle of abuse). I turned a blind eye to excuses when my jewelry would go missing or he was constantly short with rent money. I wanted to help him and to save him from his addiction. I felt needed—though anyone in a relationship with an addict knows that this feeling of being needed comes with a very chaotic, tumultuous and exhausting price tag.

The abuse was primarily emotional, mental and verbal. The drip of it was so regular that it seeped into my being and became planted into my mind and heart until I believed it. I believed that my past was so sordid that no one besides him would ever love me. I thought that I was lucky that he was staying with me. The lies that he told and I believed went on and on. I knew he had a temper, and when he was especially drunk, he'd rage on about his alcoholic, abusive father who repeatedly beat his mother. But for a long time, I never thought that he would be violent to me.

I vividly remember the first time my eyes were opened to the depths of his hatred and rage towards me. In a calm conversation at a public laundromat while we folded bath towels, he described how after we had broken up the first time, he would drive by my old apartment. When he saw my new boyfriend's truck out front, he would think about all the different ways he would kill me. He described a few options in detail just as calmly as if he were reading a grocery list. I was shocked, but unfortunately laughed it off, not sure how to react. Many times have I looked back and wished that I would have listened to my gut instead of my self-doubt and gotten out of that relationship right then.

The relationship continued to decline as it escalated into more serious offenses. The final straw was one night when I had to call the police four times in less than 18 hours. He was finally arrested and booked after he threatened the arresting officer and threatened my life in front of the police officers. The next morning, I obtained a restraining order, and I thought that I could start to breathe easier again. Unfortunately, that was not the case.

The stalking and harassment began immediately upon his release from jail. He followed me to work, showed up at my apartment and would appear wherever I happened to be around town. I did what I was told to do, and I called the police to report these incidents. He was eventually arrested for violating the restraining order and served jail time. But that experience ingrained a habit of constantly looking over my shoulder—never knowing when or where he might appear.

I moved a few states away, but I was still close enough that I could drive back to testify against him in court. I was far enough away (I thought) that I could breathe a little easier. While he was incarcerated, I received a call from my victim's advocate reporting additional threats against my life that he was making while in jail. In a panic, I asked her what to do. I couldn't have guessed her response to me.

"Go underground, go into hiding—go as deep as you can, change your name, change your appearance and cut off ties with everyone in your past so that he cannot find you. I have no doubt he will follow through on these threats, given the chance."

Imagine, at 27 years old, in a new state, only knowing three people, having escaped from a horrible relationship and attempting to heal from the trauma. Then imagine on top of that having to make the choice to leave everything and everyone behind that you've known up until that point and start from scratch. This task was monumental, especially for someone who already had a shattered self-concept. Even thought I still thought I couldn't make it on my own, that's what I had to do. I only kept in touch with my parents, my brother and three longtime friends who I knew had no connection to my ex-boyfriend nor would they ever divulge my whereabouts.

I thought I'd been at rock bottom before, but that early time of hiding out was my true breaking point. I'd never felt more alone, and I had nowhere to turn. I cried out to God—not in frustration, fear and anger as I had been doing throughout this ordeal—but in complete brokenness and repentance. I sobbed on the floor, not knowing what to do or even if God would hear me because of how I'd disgraced and defiled myself over the years. But, after crying for what seemed like hours, I laid there exhausted. It was then that I felt a small flicker—at the time, I didn't even know what it was—but *something* felt different inside. I had accepted Christ as my Savior early in high school, but had almost immediately began acting out and rebelling against Him and my perceptions of His rigid rules and requirements. I certainly hadn't been living a life pleasing to Him, and I thought surely His back would be turned from me forever.

Thankfully, God is full of mercy and grace, and He is quick to forgive a truly repentant heart. I accepted responsibility for the things I had done and the issues I had brought to that destructive relationship. I repented for those actions and for other sins in my life. I thought that now that I was on a new path that life could and would be rosy. But, one of the hardest lessons I've learned is that even though God may have forgiven me for living in sin, consequences of sin remain. Although our lives can be transformed through Him, that doesn't mean we are free from the results of our actions.

So, fast-forward a number of years. I've met and married a wonderful man, who delights in me and I in him. He knows my past and he has never judged or looked down on me. He accepts that I am hugely flawed (as we all are) and loves me in spite of it. He is supportive of my idiosyncrasies—how I always double check that the doors are locked, and the security alarm is set. I always sit with my back to a wall whenever we go out, and I constantly look over my shoulder. My husband would never dream of sneaking up on me, nor would he raise his voice or hand in anger. I feel comfortable, safe and secure, and I thank God for blessing me with the gift of this man.

My ex-boyfriend served about 18 months in jail and I had not heard from him since his release. It had now been eight years, and I had started to become just a *little* more comfortable in my surroundings, though I was especially hyperaware whenever I went out with our daughter. My life had been transformed—I was now an entrepreneur, with dreams of becoming an author. I loved God, my expanding family and my life. Sure, it was lonely at times, especially with the advent of social media. I wished I could reach out to old friends and connect with them, to hear how they were doing and share life together. But I knew that a trail could lead my ex to find me.

Early one morning, he did just that. I was out of town traveling for work and I received an email from him. Actually, there were multiple emails over the course of a few hours that were received while I slept. My heart leapt into my throat and I was paralyzed. I had no idea where my ex was sending the messages from. His notes made it very clear that he knew specific details about my husband, where he worked, where our house was, etc. Here I was—two states away from my family and eight months pregnant—and all I wanted was to be at home, holding my daughter tight and protecting her from a knock that I was sure to arrive at the door, with my ex on the other side.

The harassing emails came on a regular basis with thinly veiled threats. I was finally able to get the court to take it seriously when they saw the messages were becoming more bizarre and more frequent. In 2011, my ex agreed to a two-year no-contact order. I thought we could breathe (slightly) easier, knowing that there would be swift and exact punishment if that were to be broken. But then, the online attempts came to discredit me and my businesses. I also received multiple prank calls throughout the day and night. These instances were not enough to convince the court of any wrongdoing, but they certainly had made my guard go up again.

I've relied heavily on my faith since that night so long ago, when I felt the love of Christ surround me in a different, more meaningful way. Even while going back and forth through the court process (after the initial two-year no-contact order expired, the harassment began again, so we are back in the midst of additional court proceedings for those charges), I know that God holds my family and me in His hands.

My life is not perfect, but I am perfectly loved by a Father who has always known how this experience would shape and mold me. He also knows how I will be able to use my story to inspire, encourage and support others escaping destructive relationships. I'd love for this to all be behind us, for my ex to find the Lord and turn his life around, but no matter what God has planned, I know that I'm not alone.

Had I continued on the path I was on way back then, I'm convinced I wouldn't be alive today. But God has a purpose for my life and I am thankful that He has always remained faithful to me, even when I didn't want anything to do with Him. He has truly moved me from tears to triumph and transformed my life. I can never thank Him enough for His grace, mercy and blessings.

DEVASTATION FROM DOMESTIC VIOLENCE REDEEMED

By Cheryl Moses

Being such a young child and losing your mother by way of domestic homicide has to be one of the most—if not the most—devastating experiences to go through. It's something you never forget, and it's also something you have to live with for the rest of your life. This tragedy changed my whole life, and every bit of emotion and pain that I experienced because of it, was for a purpose. I had not recognized that purpose—until now.

My mother was murdered by my father when I was 10 years old. We lived in Long Island, New York, at the time. After this horrific event happened, I had to go and live with my Aunt Mae, my mother's sister, in New York City. It wasn't the best living situation, because my aunt was nothing like my mom. It was a trying time, but I stayed with her until I turned 18 years old, when she told me to leave her home.

At that time, I had a boyfriend, who was in and out of prison. He was a bad boy and I was a good girl who liked bad boys. After living with his mom for a few months, I got my own apartment with him and I ended up getting pregnant shortly after I moved in. I also became a victim of domestic violence, both physically and emotionally during the pregnancy. He was involved with drug activity and he brought it into my home. I remember being four months pregnant and having my apartment door pushed in, getting knocked upside my head with a gun, and having and a knife to my throat—all because of his actions. It felt like I was going through the same things that I saw my mother go through, and my life was so difficult that I got to a point where I just wanted to die. The pregnancy is what saved me from going through with suicide.

Shortly after my daughter was born, her father ended up going back to prison for about six years. During that time, I moved to the Bronx, and started getting close to someone else who seemed like he was a pretty decent guy. He helped me with my baby girl, and he supported me when she wasn't thriving at three months old and went into foster care. He wasn't abusive like my previous boyfriend, but I later realized that he was a pathological liar and a thief. I stuck it out on and off for a few years with him until I just couldn't take it anymore. I'm not sure of why I dealt with him for so long. I guess that I didn't want to be alone or perhaps I thought that he would change one day.

I did everything that I was supposed to do to get my daughter back home with me. After a couple of years, I relocated to Ohio to go to college for nursing and to find some peace in my life. I set goals, and I was taking action to achieve them. I received a job as an EKG technician in a hospital, and things were going really well.

When I was in my second year of college, my daughter's father was released from prison, and we began to talk again. He was very convincing when he talked about changing his ways. He actually did change—for a little while. I forgave him and we started to build a relationship again. This reconciliation was something I had always wanted because my daughter, who was six years old at the time, deserved to have her father around. I was also tired of being a single mom.

After a couple of years of dating again, we decided to get married. It didn't feel right when it was time to say, "I do," but I did it anyway—despite what my intuition was telling me. Two weeks after the wedding, I ended up having a miscarriage, which was very disappointing. What was even more disappointing was the fact that my husband started going back to his old ways. He wasn't physically abusive, but he was still emotionally abusive. He wasn't working or doing anything with his life, he was drinking daily, and he seemed to be depressed. I, on the other hand, was working a full time job and taking classes to get into the nursing program. Having him around was more than like having another kid living in the house.

I found myself crying constantly, asking God to release me from this mess that I had caused in my life. I took full responsibility for my decisions. It hurt me deeply when my nine-year-old daughter came in the room after he finished yelling, kissed me on the forehead and told me "It will be ok." It took me back to when I would comfort my mom after she had a fight with my dad. I was fed up and wanted a divorce. I also had fear that I would end up like my mom if I did not change this situation.

What I didn't know was that my husband was living a double life, per se. He had been involved in drug and other criminal activity. He got caught, and had used his malicious ways to get my name mixed up in his wrong doing as well. I ended up having a case brought against me because of his actions, even though I didn't know what he was up to. He was taken into custody by law enforcement, and I filed for a divorce. At the same time, I was going back and forth to court, trying to prove my innocence.

Who would ever think that their own husband would do this to them? So many thoughts were racing through my mind as to why this happened to me, but I still couldn't figure it out. After everything else that I had been through in my life, I thought God just hated me, and maybe that hatred was the reason for this tragedy.

Not too long before all of this took place, my dad had been released from prison after serving about 17 years. I was pleased to know that he was now a born again Christian, and that he had received Christ as his Lord and Savior. I started to build a relationship with him and leaned on him to help me get through my own situation. He even decided to take a few days off from work, and he drove down to see my in Ohio from New York, just to be supportive.

This case against me became the pivotal moment in my life. I was being accused of something that I did not know was going on, and no one could help me but God. I began to diligently seek Him at this point, to get some answers. I always had a relationship with God, but this time it was different. In my heart, I knew that something else—more than just the trying events— was going on. I began to wonder and ask God, *Why me? Why now?* I had just gotten accepted into a nursing program, which I had worked hard for, my household was at peace, my daughter was happy, and my future was looking great—now that my husband was out of my life.

One of the first things I did, was talk to my "spiritual" mom, whom we called Ma Tyler. She was known around town and in the churches as being able to speak to and hear God directly. I figured if anyone could give me some kind of message, it would be her. I learned so much during my first visit with her. She was speaking to God and He was speaking right back to her in front of me. He told her about the suicidal thoughts when I was younger and about what happened when I was 10 years old. I had never shared any of this information with her previously.

She talked to me at first, and then she let me know that God said to her that He hears my cries. She also said that He was going to *"take my tears and bottle them up."* That message still makes me cry to this day. She also asked, "You hear God, don't you?" I told her "yes" because sometimes I did hear Him speak to me. She then took me into her prayer room, covered me with a prayer cloth and began to pray. My body started to sway as the tears continued to roll down my face. She let me know that God was speaking to me at that time.

When I spoke to her about the situation I was going through, she couldn't tell me what the outcome was going to be, because she said that she regularly asked God to not let her see how situations will end. I believed her and didn't press her anymore about my circumstances. I was nervous though, and it was extremely hard to shake off those fears.

Before I left her home, she gave me some instructions, which included recording my dreams, setting my radio to a Christian station and letting it play all day, going on a fast for the weekend, and reading *Total Forgiveness* by R. T. Kendall.

I went home and later on that night, a demonic force came over me when I was trying to sleep. As I lay awake in my bed, I began to feel paralyzed, and I could not move. My eyes were open but my body was not moving at all. I heard a grungy dark noise and darkness came over my eyes. All I could do is say, "Jesus" over and over and over until this force went away. I did not allow the Devil to win

I did everything Ma Tyler told me to. The book blessed me in many ways because I was now looking at forgiveness in a totally different way. I realized that I had not forgiven my dad like I needed to, and now I needed to forgive my soon to be ex-husband. When I went back to see her, I told her about my experience that night, and she told me that the Devil was trying to scare me. Every time I went to see her, something dreadful would happen after our visit. The Enemy did not want me doing this work, and it was obvious.

I'll never forget, Ma Tyler gave me a scripture to read for what I was going through: "Trust in the Lord with all your heart; do not depend on your own understanding. Seek his will in all you do, and he will direct your paths" (Proverbs 3:5–6, NKJV). I read that scripture over and over again. Another sister in Christ gave me this verse: "And we know that God causes everything to work together for the good of those who love God and are called according to his purpose for them" (Romans 8:28, NLT), These two scriptures began to make sense to me as time went on.

As for that case, I ended up receiving three years of probation, which wasn't as bad as the house arrest they had talked about. I still remember the probation officer coming to my house to prepare me for the house arrest. As she was talking, God said, "The Devil is a liar." I heard it clear as day. When they cleared me of house arrest and settled on a lesser punishment, I knew that the voice I had heard was God.

During this time I had also began seeing someone who had been a friend who I had known for a few years. I was quite skeptical about him since my past relationships had been so horrible. He seemed to be really nice and supportive, especially since we both had been experiencing challenges in our lives.

To top it all off, I suffered an ectopic pregnancy, which almost killed me. I didn't know that I was pregnant, and then one day my tube exploded causing me to bleed internally. I was in an extreme amount of pain, and I did not know what was going on. I kept blacking out on and off for most of the day until I gained enough strength to call someone to take me to the hospital. My blood pressure was very low because I had lost so much blood. The pain felt like someone was sticking me with needles all over my body. When they sent me to the rest room to give a urine sample, I blacked out again and woke up on the floor not knowing what had happened. They immediately sent me to emergency surgery, to have the tube removed. I was devastated. My chances of having another child had been ruined. I couldn't help but think that I was being punished for something yet again.

I ended up doing two semesters of nursing school, but then I had to let that dream go. The stress, the case, the divorce and losing my job were all weighing on me heavily. And now my chances of being a nurse were ruined. It was hard for me to accept that all those years of going to school just to get into a nursing program had been tarnished at this point and had been in vain. It took a long time for me to stop crying about it.

Despite my tears and disappointment, I continued to diligently seek God. The one thing that kept me holding on was the fact that God had never failed me. I made some bad decisions, and I felt like I went through hell in my past, but God never let me fall so hard that I could not recover. When I think back about the pregnancy, I felt no fear as I went into surgery. I also felt that I must still be on this earth for a purpose because I'm still breathing despite how bad that situation was. After all of these trials, it was time for me to figure out what my purpose was and get to work to make it happen.

I had the desire to move forward, but I had no money coming in. I didn't know what I was going to do. Fortunately, my dad stepped in and became my backbone financially, even though our relationship seemed to be withering away. This blessing was something else that I couldn't understand. I later found out that my day had been diagnosed with Post Traumatic Stress Disorder from serving in the Vietnam War. This diagnosis answered some of the questions that had been lingering in my mind, especially about his actions in the past.

After I spoke with different people and seeking answers to the question, "What am I going to do now?" I started to gain an interest in a number of things, ultimately choosing the path of entrepreneurship. This route was scary for me because I had always wanted to have my own business, but I never had the confidence or faith to take that leap.

When I was trying to figure all of this out, I got pregnant again. I was shocked. The pregnancy was successful and God blessed me with a healthy and beautiful baby boy, who I named Caleb. A son was a gift I had always wanted. He was a miracle in my eyes. I finally received what I had wished for. Things were starting to evolve for me.

As I went along my journey, there were a couple of things that took place: First, I realized that when I lost my job, it was God closing the door for me to pursue something greater. I remember having a patient, who I had never seen before, ask me if I was happy with my job. When I told her "no," she said, "You should do what's going to make you happy. If this isn't where you want to be, then it's time to move on. I don't know if I'm here to tell you this message." The next day that patient was discharged. I never forgot our conversation, and I believe those doors were closed for a reason. Second, God started giving me the vision of what He wanted me to do. Not only did He want me to do great things in business, He wanted me to serve for a purpose. My mess is supposed to be my message to other single moms who have been through domestic violence and torn down spiritually.

Losing a parent at such a young age is devastating for any child. It took me 20 years to forgive my father. He took my mom away from me and he took himself away from me. The feeling of abandonment and loneliness is a void that is very hard to fill.

God also showed me that I was to start a nonprofit organization for kids who experienced that same tragedy that I experienced. These kids who go through the program will integrate successfully in society by honing in on their creativity through dance, music, writing and art. They will also have mentoring to help them break through their pain, emotions, and feelings. The organization's goal is to develop young girls into leaders of tomorrow by restoring their hope and allowing them to discover their innate strengths so they can prosper in love and life.

I'm also in a great position on my journey to provide business training and coaching to help single moms so they can live a better quality of life and follow their hearts' desires.

When I sit back and look at all that God has put in my heart to do and how He has changed my point of view on so many things, it really blows my mind. I never in a million years thought that I would someone who could make an impact on so many lives. I'm not worried about the future or how things will unfold and come together, I just know that they will. My confidence is because I trust God and because He has made me the righteousness of God. I also know that when God closes doors, He has something greater in His plan.

I believe that God has bottled up my tears and that He continues to do so even now. This journey hasn't been easy, but as my dad would say, "Anything worth having is worth working hard for."

IN THE ARMS OF THE SHEPHERD

By Kayla Fioravanti

When I was very young, straggling behind the others, out of
my youthfulness I was stolen in the night
By the Enemy of all.
I became disoriented and confused, lost.
I wandered deeper and deeper
Into the vast wilderness around me.
I could hear the Shepherd calling,
Feel His footsteps near me, but
I could not find my way to Him.
It seemed as though the darkness
Would separate us for all of eternity.

I wandered farther into the wilderness, and
In the darkness I became blinded.
The depth of my emptiness consumed and paralyzed me.
I was drowning in my own total despair.
I became cast, totally helpless,
Weighed down by my own hurt, anger and filth.

When my body could move no further
The Shepherd called again. He was near.
I could run no further away, go no deeper into myself.
Body and soul, I laid down helpless at His feet.
Exhausted, empty and consumed with guilt.

I could feel the Shepherd reaching out to heal me.
I turned into His support and surrendered completely.

He restored me, healed my soul, cleansed my body.
He lifted me tenderly into His loving embrace
And covered me with His amazing grace.
He healed me, renewed me.

My overgrown coat had been laden
with guilt, dirt and shame.
Yet as He took His place at the throne of my heart,
And I released myself into Him,
It all fell away and scattered as far as East is from West.

I was free—In His arms
I became white as snow.

The all-consuming emptiness
Was all at once filled with His presence,
And I was totally satisfied, finally longed for nothing else.
I had found my way home, The Shepherd, my Savior
Was the remedy I had sought in the darkest of days.

He restores my soul in every present day.
When I am burdened, I lay my worries at His feet and
Crawl up into His mighty lap and rest.
I surrender each day to His will, and am comforted

By His very presence. My Shepherd,

My Savior whispers in my ear,

And I can hear Him now. I know where He is.

He is here, always here.

He lives in me.

The poem *In the Arms of the Shepherd* tells my life story. I don't often speak of the moments in my life that filled me with shame and misdirected me. However, at eight years old while frolicking through life, I very suddenly experienced a hurt and shame so deep that it changed the course of my life. A babysitter abused me. I overheard him blame me. I took the blame to heart, and the "Enemy of all" used it to confuse and disorient me. I believe Satan is the Enemy of all and the great deceiver.

From that period of my life onward, I could feel and sense a darkness that I had never known before. From within the darkness, I changed directions in life onto a path leading me deeper and deeper into the wilderness. As early as I can remember, I was always seeking God. A veil of darkness blurred my vision. I listened to the world around me and found myself running. I grew further from God despite an echo of His voice making me want to seek Him.

As the years passed, I entered my teen years seeking to fill a void that I felt was ever present in my life. I filled the emptiness with alcohol and parties. I put myself in dangerous positions fueled by mind-altering and inhibition-numbing drunkenness. I ended up being used and taken advantage of, leaving me feeling paralyzed by guilt and shame.

The party abruptly ended when I was 25 years old. One morning, with no memory of the night before, I awoke feeling life inside of me. The feeling of life was foreign and altogether consuming, because I had been so dead and so numb for so very long. I knew with certainty that I was pregnant. Just as suddenly, I also knew life began at conception and I had to protect this new life with all of my being.

I was only hours pregnant when I chose to stop drinking for the good of my child. I had studied fetal alcohol syndrome in college and couldn't bear to injure this baby. I was instantly converted from being pro-choice to being ready to sacrifice everything to protect life, especially this life. My future plans to obtain my Ph.D. were quickly abandoned. They now become meaningless in the face of this new life.

I went to the store a week later to buy a pregnancy test and bottle of wine. I decided one or the other would be my future. The test came up positive, so I gave the bottle of wine to my neighbors. The next day I went to confirm the test at a women's clinic. I stood beside the nurse waiting for the test results. It came up negative.

I insisted that I was indeed pregnant. She administered another more accurate test. This one came up with a very faint positive sign. The nurse turned to me and said, "Don't worry. It is early enough we can get this taken care of before you even know you're pregnant." I suddenly realized the women's clinic I had gone to for help was, in reality, an abortion clinic. I flew out of there never looking back.

Later that day in downtown Portland, I told the biological father that I was pregnant. We had been friends for a lifetime, so I felt safe as I told him. He turned to me and said, "Don't worry, I will be there...for the abortion." My resolve to protect my child grew. I settled in for a battle as pressure to abort my child continued to come from every direction.

Those around pressured me daily with arguments like, "I never chose to be a father" and "Having this baby will ruin your life." For the first time, I realized I had been playing Russian roulette with my life, making choices that caused the creation of children. I also knew this new choice would save my life. I didn't know how, but I knew this child was a life preserver. Another argument proposed to me was, "It would be better to have an abortion than to live with this mistake forever. At the very least, consider adoption and get on with your life."

And at 25, with a college degree—world travels already under my belt—I knew that for me, adoption wasn't the best option. I was willing and able to let go of the future I had planned to grasp hold of the hope of a new future. I never wrestled with the decision to abort my baby because I knew I would never recover from it. I did take the time to wrestle with the decision of adoption.

Someone close to me said, "But you don't even like children." To this statement, I answered, "But I love this one."

I realized everything about my life was wrong. I went out searching in earnest for God. I searched church after church and denomination after denomination. I wanted to either prove the Bible as true or the whole Bible as false. In my mind, there could no longer be any half-truths.

Jesus either was the "way, the truth and the light," or He wasn't. Growing up, priests taught me that the Bible was full of myths that God used to teach us lessons. These thought spun me further into confusion. In the midst of my search, I quite clearly heard the message, *"For all have sinned and fall short of the glory of God"* (Romans 3:23).

All my running, all my blaming and all my confusion ended with the realization that I am a sinner. We are all sinners. We all fall short of His glory. And at that moment, with that realization, I surrendered my life and gained a whole new life. *"But when the kindness and love of God our Savior appeared, He saved us, not because of righteous things we had done, but because of His mercy. He saved us through the washing of rebirth and renewal by the Holy Spirit, whom He poured out on us generously through Jesus Christ our Savior, so that, having been justified by His grace, we might become heirs having the hope of eternal life"* (Titus 3:4–7).

I was pregnant, single and "heavy laden." I hit bottom and was downcast. However, instead of leaving me to suffer the consequences of my life, Jesus found me in the wilderness and He tenderly rescued me. *"Suppose one of you has a hundred sheep and loses one of them. Doesn't he leave the ninety-nine in the open country and go after the lost sheep until he finds it? And when he finds it, he joyfully puts it on his shoulders and goes home. Then he calls his friends and neighbors together and says, 'Rejoice with me; I have found my lost sheep'"* (Luke 15:4–6).

I was the one lost sheep before He found me. Then, I was free—In His arms.

I became white as snow. *"'Come now, let us reason together,' says the LORD. 'Though your sins are like scarlet, they shall be as white as snow; though they are red as crimson, they shall be like wool'"* (Isaiah 1:18. ESV).

God had restored my broken life. It would be a mistake to infer that my life became painless and carefree. In reality, challenges could have buried me alive, especially in my early years as a Christian. God gave me enough faith for each step forward. When the burdens of being responsible to answer to God for my actions alone were lifted from me, I was suddenly stronger than ever. I was fortified by the promises of God. I was confident of the sureness that Jesus will be standing before me when I come face to face with judgment. On that day, I will covered in His perfect blood. *"God made him who had no sin to be sin for us, so that in him we might become the righteousness of God"* (2 Corinthians 5:21, NIV).

Education, partying, people and travel never quenched my thirst for a purpose bigger than myself. Nothing satisfies the soul like surrender to Christ. I do not deserve His grace and love, but He gives it freely to anyone who asks. The problem that God solved, through Jesus Christ, is my separation from God. He is perfect and I am sinful.

Becoming a Christian simply meant that I recognized myself as flawed, sinful and broken. I came to the solid realization that God's way is best for me. I stopped resisting Him. God created us. Our souls exist for the singular purpose of being filled by Christ. The unique act of Christianity is to surrender, handing our lives fully to God. It is to die to ourselves—to worldly desires—and to trust God's perfect plan. When I surrendered, He filled me with indescribable joy, unquenchable hope and meaningful purpose as I express His love through my life.

All of us have a God-shaped vacuum in the center of who we are. Our souls are meant to be filled by Christ. The truth is that we are all sinners separated from God. The truth is that Jesus bridges the separation. He is our salvation.

We only need to surrender. *Why do I tell you this?* Because through the years I have asked a million unanswered questions to Christians as I was seeking to understand what was so different about their faith. What was so special about their relationship with Jesus Christ? No one had the courage to answer my questions. If you have questions and you want the answer, continue reading.

Are you surrendered? Will you stop right where you are and give the Lord everything, all of it, even the parts you are hanging onto in the deep recesses of your mind? The steps of surrender are quite simple.

1. Recognize that you are a sinner. *"All have sinned and fall short of the glory of God"* (Romans 3:23, NIV) and *"Salvation is found in no one else, for there is no other name under heaven given to mankind by which we must be saved"* (Acts 4:12, NIV).

2. Realize human works cannot make us holy before God. *"The wages of sin is death, but the gift of God is eternal life in Christ Jesus our Lord"* (Romans 6:23, NIV) Salvation is a free gift. *"For all have sinned and fall short of the glory of God, and all are justified freely by his grace through the redemption that came by Christ Jesus"* (Romans 3:23–24, ESV).

3. Rely totally on Jesus Christ alone for your salvation. *"For God so loved the world that he gave his one and only Son, that whoever believes in him shall not perish but have eternal life"* (John 3:16, NIV) and *"All those the Father gives me will come to me, and whoever comes to me I will never drive away"* (John 6:37, NIV).

4. Pray the prayer below or cry out in your own words to God. *"But what does it say? "The word is near you; it is in your mouth and in your heart," that is, the message concerning faith that we proclaim: If you declare with your mouth, "Jesus is Lord," and believe in your heart that God raised him from the dead, you will be saved. For it is with your heart that you believe and are justified, and it is with your mouth that you profess your faith and are saved. As Scripture says, "Anyone who believes in him will never be put to shame." For there is no difference between Jew and Gentile—the same Lord is Lord of all and richly blesses all who call on him, for, "Everyone who calls on the name of the Lord will be saved"* (Romans 10:8–13, NIV).

If this message resonates with you, and you want to commit your life to Jesus, you can pray the suggested prayer below. If you still have questions, you can pray and ask God to show you that He's real. You might also want to read the book of John in the Bible. This book will give you more insight about Jesus.

Prayer: Dear God, I come to you in the name of Jesus. I admit to You that I am a sinner. I am sorry for my sins and the life I have lived. I need your forgiveness. I believe Jesus Christ died for my sins, was resurrected and lives at the right hand of the Father. Please wash me clean from all my sin, shame, and guilt. Take up residence in my life, as my Lord, King and Savior. Thank you for giving me the gift of eternal life and the assurance that You will never leave me. Amen.

Next Step: Find a church where you can celebrate your new relationship with God and where you can grow in faith. It's important the church teaches directly from the Bible. It's also important you start reading the Bible on your own, too. This is how you'll nurture your personal relationship with Jesus and it'll give you discernment. It's important to always verify what you hear being taught by others with your own study of the scriptures. You can pray God will help you grow and He will help you find the best church for you.

I would also suggest you start with these three books of the Bible in this order: The Gospel of John, Romans and Philippians. Then you should talk to the pastor in the church that you find. Ask to be baptized, which is something the Lord told His followers to do as an act of obedience and a public profession of the faith that you now claim as your own.

This is just the beginning of a life-long journey. You will find many resources to help you grow in your faith. Talk to your pastor, get plugged into a small group Bible study and know your eternal salvation has just been ensured.

EMBRACING EXTRAORDINARY CALLINGS

AND LET THERE BE LIGHT!
By Dr. Lori M. Hobson

When I was four, my mother, determined that I would not be clumsy, enrolled me in a dance school. I took ballet and tap lessons every Saturday morning. My teacher was a former Radio City Music Hall Rockette, and she was a real tough cookie. She wore platinum blonde hair, red lipstick and high-heeled tap shoes. One very consistent thing about her was, no matter how much she yelled at you in class, you got a kiss from her as you left.

Our teacher did not have just run of the mill dance recitals—she had shows with themes. I remember that one year we performed *New York, New York* and another year we did another Broadway show. But the year that I will always remember the most was when I was seven years old, and the theme was *South Pacific*, a Broadway play from 1949 that had also become a popular movie.

Before starting class one day, our teacher gathered us together and asked, "Who wants to do a solo?" Without hesitation, I stepped forward and raised my hand. "I do," I said. I was given the song "Honey Bun" from *South Pacific*. The song features lyrics like "Get a load of honey bun tonight" and "Every inch is packed with dynamite," which the audience found hilarious coming from a seven-year-old girl. They laughed when I sang those lines and I had no idea why—but I really didn't care. I was doing something that I enjoyed and the audience was entertained. Most of all, I never once thought that they were laughing at me or making fun of me.

At the next year's recital, people recognized me and asked what I was doing that year. I remember being a little surprised that people knew who I was. I performed at every recital until I was 12 years old, when my teacher was killed in a car accident. When that tragedy happened, I went to another dance school, where my classmates were unaware of how long I'd been dancing. I was praised often by my new teachers and called on to demonstrate certain moves. However, my new classmates resented me and would say mean things to or about me whenever they got a chance. As a result, I gave up something that I considered my absolute favorite thing to do—dancing.

That was my first of many experiences that taught me to keep part of myself hidden so that people would not be mean to me. I wasn't being true to myself, but it was safe. Eventually I lost sight of that bold seven-year-old girl, who volunteered to stand out without fear or hesitation. Occasionally, I would think of my younger self and wonder where she went. Little did I know—that bold little girl never went anywhere. She was hanging out waiting for me to learn enough about myself to acknowledge her.

God's Word says, *"What you're after is truth from the inside out. Enter me, then; conceive a new, true life"* (Psalm 51:6, The Message). After I sought and was blessed with a personal, unique relationship with my Lord and Savior, I began my journey to rediscover that bold, beautiful, talented little girl.

Two things predicated my reconnecting with the bodacious, unapologetic performer in me. First after suffering numerous, undeserved attacks from people for no apparent reason, I realized that I could not control the actions of those people or anyone else. Second, I accepted the fact that I have a light that makes me stand out no matter what I do. My light attracts most people. It makes them want to talk to me and/or be in my presence. Unfortunately, a tiny percentage of the population—although attracted to my light—want to put it out. I can't do anything about their actions.

So I decided to embrace my light. That led me to a more through understanding of another passage of Scripture. *"You are the light of the world. A city on a hill cannot be hidden. Neither do people light a lamp and put it under a bowl. Instead they put it on its stand, and it gives light to everyone in the house"* (Matthew 5:14–15, NIV).

Now, my bold little girl resides inside an even bolder, grown woman. I am completely, confidently, authentically who I am. You couldn't put my light out if you used a fire hose. It feels like someone let me of a cage and locked the door behind me. The best part of that unleashed feeling comes out three to five days a week during cardiovascular work out, which—you guessed it—is dance. Please understand, I still have my share of challenges, but the feeling of accepting who I am is indescribable! It is amazing—and it is something that I must share with others!

My life coaching business is built around this premise. That is why my tag line is "I will be President of Your Fan Club Until You Can Take Over." Nevertheless, the life coach in me cannot end this chapter without offering you scriptural encouragement.

On the difficult days when my little performer is threatening to go back into isolation, I go to these passages of scripture:

- *"For I know the plans I have for you," declares the LORD, "plans to prosper you and not to harm you, plans to give you hope and a future"* (Jeremiah 29:11, NIV).

and

- *"Therefore do not cast away your confidence, which has great reward. For you have need of endurance, so that after you have done the will of God, you may receive the promise"* (Hebrews 10:35–36, NKJV).

Regardless of your age, when you begin to walk in God's purpose for your life, you will encounter people who want to put out your light. It is important for you to remember that the light given to you by God is meant to shine. Unfortunately, the more you shine them more "haters" you attract. Some of them will be people who are close to you. God wants you to recognize your haters for what they are. It's hard to realize that they can sometimes be people who are close to you. Continuing to shine may involve setting boundaries or even severing ties with people who are trying to block your blessings. This boundary-setting process will be challenging but completely worth it. Let your light shine!

COUNTING MY BLESSINGS
By Dr. Esly Carvalho

"For the Lord is good and his love endures forever" (Psalm 100: 5, NIV).

Since I am writing this article on the eve of Thanksgiving, I thought I would share with you some of the things for which I'm thankful. Some of them may surprise you, as they did me, when I began to think over what I would like to tell you.

I'd like to start by saying that I am grateful for *my name*. I haven't always been grateful about that. After my parents immigrated to Dallas from Brazil, the first day of school was always a challenge, to say the least. When the teacher stopped roll call at the letter "C," I knew what was coming. I always seemed to stick out. Why couldn't I have a name that others could at least pronounce? I once made a comment about it to my mom, and that's when I realized that *my name* was one of my greatest blessings.

She told me that my first name came from one of the "begats" in the genealogy of Jesus (told in Luke 3:25), and that my name means, "God is at your side." I often remembered those words as I faced a difficult childhood. It comforted me to know that every time someone called out my name, they were saying, "God is at your side!" Many years later, I read in a Bible dictionary that my name means, "whom Jehovah has reserved," and I realized that my name was also a confirmation of God's calling in my life. I am grateful that God has reserved me for Himself, for His ministry and for His service.

I never thought much about my last name until my Brazilian grandmother told me that it meant "oak tree" in Portuguese. A few years ago, God asked me what I wanted to do for the next 20 years of my life! I asked Him for some time to think and pray about it. About six months later, I heard a friend preach about Luke 4, where Jesus quotes Isaiah 61.

Here is just a portion of that passage:

"The Spirit of the Lord is upon Me,
Because He has anointed Me
To preach the gospel to the poor;
He has sent Me to heal the brokenhearted,[j]
To proclaim liberty to the captives...(Luke4:18, NKJV)

As I prayed and read that passage, I realized that God had written that chapter just for me.

As a psychotherapist, the words of that chapter were a perfect job description... so I got on my knees and I started reading it back to God. I told Him, "Lord, this is what I want to do for the next 20 years of my life." And then I hit Isaiah 61:3, where it says that we would be like "oaks of righteousness!" ("carvalhos de justiça").

I'm grateful for growing up in this country. Although I never felt like I fit in, my schooling here gave me special gifts that have enabled me to serve God and His people. Since I learned to speak English as an American (or better, as a Texan!), it opened the doors to many opportunities and experiences that I would never have had without it. I attended a professional school and became a licensed psychologist after my parents returned to Brazil. I was also hired as an executive bilingual secretary to the Greek Ambassador, a job that paid my way through school. I had to lose my Texas drawl real fast to succeed, but that job got me through!

I'm grateful to the Lord for my family. On one hand, I have the unique privilege of being a sixth-generation born-again Christian in Brazil! I can still remember my great-grandmother reading the Bible on the front porch of the house. I can remember my grandparents drawing us all together to pray for us and for our safety. I can remember what it cost us to be non-Catholic Christians in the largest Roman Catholic country in the world. Today, 15% of the Brazilian population is born-again Christian, and that group is growing. That translates into 26 million people who now confess Jesus as Savior.

On the other hand, I found out that this multi-generational Christian legacy did not guard me against the woes of a dysfunctional family. My father slowly fell away from the Lord as I grew up, and he was an alcoholic for more than 30 years. I grew up in a crazy-making family that drove me straight into the arms of Jesus at age 15. I learned that Jesus could get me through anything—and He did.

I'm grateful for God's calling on my life. When I was 17, the Lord called me into the ministry of reconciliation through the passage in Luke, as I mentioned earlier. I started seminary and psychology school together. I quickly learned that the Christians were convinced I had bought my one-way ticket to hell because they had seen so many Christians in psychology school leave the church. My psychology colleagues told me point-blank that I would never amount to much as a therapist because I was religious. I praise the Lord for the fiery furnace that tested my faith and led me to the decision to become the best possible therapist for the glory of God. I made a decision back then that my professional life had to reflect the excellence of God, and I have let that principle guide me ever since that time.

I'm also grateful for my divorce. Although I am not a proponent of divorce, God freed me from a terrible mistake and an abusive marriage. That great tragedy in my life became a blessing many years later in a my book, *When the Bond Breaks*, which was also published in Spanish and Portuguese.

I have a friend who says that our books are our little missionaries, and they go where we can't. I know this statement is true. People from Cuba have told me how the book has helped them through their own experiences. Because there are no accessible photocopying machines, it is not uncommon to go to Cuba and find that people have painstakingly written portions of books by hand so they could have copies for themselves.

I know that God has used my story of recovery from divorce to help other women survive the pain of betrayal and abuse, especially as Christian women in the church of Latin America. There, divorced women in church are treated as second-class citizens; they may not be allowed to stand and pray out loud in church because they are divorced.

I'm also grateful for my only child, Raquel. She has given me a small glimpse of what it means to love unconditionally and to learn from the wisdom and innocence of little children. I learned that the love of God was so great that He could sacrifice His only child to redeem others. That act is something I don't think I could ever do. I cannot imagine giving up the life of my only child so that other people—bad people—could have a chance at eternal life.

I am grateful to God, who gives second chances. I thought my ministry life was over and that I was useless to the Lord after my divorce. That and other painful experiences that I have gone through have made me more sensitive to the pain of others. I have learned to listen to my patients with my heart, not just my ears. I am so unworthy—and yet—God has brought me opportunities and blessings above and beyond anything I could have ever imagined, much less deserved.

I am also so grateful for my second husband, Ken, who has loved me as Christ loves the church. He also lays his life down for me. I live in an unusual household. Ken was raised in China and spoke Mandarin as his first language, although he has forgotten it now. He lived in Ecuador for 33 years as a missionary. We speak three languages at home—all the time! My daughter once asked if she would ever have a normal life. I answered, of course not! You don't even have a normal mother!

I am so thankful for the stability that Ken has brought into my life. I didn't question whether or not I would follow him when his transfer to Dallas became a reality. I walked away from so many things that gave significance to my life in Ecuador to follow the life partner that God has given me. I walked away from my practice, my patients, my friends, a comfortable lifestyle, people who were slowly being won to the Lord and my only child. But Ken has been my greatest fan, my most ardent supporter and a kind and loving parent to my daughter. There are debts in life that no amount of love can pay back. I am indebted to Ken forever.

Finally, I am grateful to a God who asks for everything, but holds nothing back. I have had to come back to the basic questions of the Christian faith in this last year: *Is God good?* Yes! Oh, yes! His goodness is abundant and His mercies are new every morning. *Is God's way perfect?* Yes! He makes our way perfect even when we wander off His beaten path. He nudges us back into the city of refuge of obedience, and He tenderly speaks to our hearts.

God has consoled me, given me hope when there was nothing left, healed my broken heart under His gentle wings, and spurred me on to dream great things for His Kingdom. Does God make sense to me? Not at all, but having come to know His heart, that doesn't matter any more. What matters now is to know Him and to glorify Him forever, with a heart full of gratitude.

I pray the following prayer based on Isaiah 61 and Luke 4 often. I encourage you to make it your prayer as well.

May the Spirit of the Sovereign Lord be upon all of us.

May the Lord anoint all of us to preach good news to the poor. I pray that He will send all of us out to bind up the broken-hearted, to proclaim freedom for the captives and release from darkness for the prisoners.

May we proclaim the year of the Lord's favor, and the day of vengeance of our God.

May we comfort those who mourn and provide for those who grieve in Zion.

I pray that God will bestow on us all a crown of beauty instead of ashes, the oil of gladness instead of a spirit of despair and depression.

May we be called oaks of righteousness, a planting of the Lord, for the display of His splendor.

Amen.

DYING TO SELF ON EARTH
By Mary Humphrey

I have adored Jesus Christ for as long as I can remember, so I have many stories to tell. As I considered which one to bring to this book, not one stood out above the others. I am a writer, which often leads me to define the meaning of words, such as, testimonial: something given or done to show gratitude or appreciation.

I begin this story of praise with my childhood. I adored The Lord, "Jesus loves me. Yes He does, for the Bible tells me so." I sang these words to my dolls, while I was riding my bicycle and as I flitted in carefree dance across the back yard of our home. I whispered words of devotion as I strolled across the fields and hiked through the woods. It was in those nature-filled places where I felt the utmost presence of God.

My mother loved The Lord, even though she was not a frequent church attender, and she did not teach her Christian walk to me. I had a father that did not love or trust The Lord, at all. Regardless, I trekked to Sunday school alone with eagerness every week, with love and immense joy in my heart. Today, I know that God stood by me as I developed from a child to a woman. I am immensely grateful that he never let go of me. He held my hand. He was, and is, my protector and comforter.

Let the little children come to me, and do not hinder them, for the kingdom of God belongs to such as these. Truly I tell you, anyone who will not receive the kingdom of God like a little child will never enter it. (Mark 10:14–15, NIV)

I gave my life to The Lord when I became a young adult. After a series of intense setbacks and disappointments, coupled with my personal struggles to understand His Word, along with not having the knowledge to seek His counsel, I allowed sin to creep into my immature Christian life. The feeling that I could no longer reach him was heartbreaking. The barrier of sin was between me and the One that had always been present. I searched for resolve through believers, and even though they tried to guide me, I received no answers that helped me step back into my life with Christ. Sleepless nights followed, as I believed I was lost for eternity.

Listen to my word, Lord, consider my lament. Hear my cry for help, my King and my God, for to you I pray. (Psalm 5:1–2, NIV)

I then met my best friend. He is now my husband. Something had changed in my heart, but I was not yet aware of the transformation. All that I understood was that, I saw my wrongs, and I wanted to make them right. I got down on my knees and prayed with my entire being, "Father, I am so sorry. I have strayed. This person, this man, needs a friend as much as I do. I want to be the best companion that he has ever known. I have set my damaging ways aside. I do not want to let him down, as I have let you down. I repent for these sins, Father. I have changed. Father, I love you so very much. I am Your daughter. In Jesus' name, Amen."

Produce fruit in keeping with repentance. (Luke 3:8, NIV)

My life filled with warmth and comfort. My husband handed me the gift of a study Bible, which provided clarity to my understanding. I began to drink in The Word as if I had come out of the desert. The Bible was life sustaining water...and truly, this is what it is...it is life giving.

But whoever is united with the Lord is one with him in spirit. (1 Corinthians 6:17, NIV)

Several years later, The Holy Spirit pressed on me that I would lead others to Jesus, and that my own written words were a part of His plan. Following this revelation, I went into a state of denial. How could he choose me to do this? I felt that I was not equipped. Once I accepted the calling, my thoughts of denial then turned to a sense of feeling singled out, special and gifted. No person in my life had ever said to me, "I hear God's voice." Yet, I heard His voice, in Spirit. I believed I was set apart from the rest. How else could I hear him answer my prayers? Why else would God have chosen me to do the things for him that I felt I was not capable or worthy of doing?

For the Mighty One has done great things for me — holy is his name. (Luke 1:49, NIV)

My work in life has taken several curves and twists since that initial day when I sensed The Lord's divine words. I now know The Truth. He gives us gifts so that he can work through us. These gifts serve one purpose, to enlarge his kingdom. We (I) am humbled, as we know it is him in us working, and it has nothing to do with self.

The key that opens the door to an intense understanding of the Lord is a relationship with Him. It is not about going to Heaven; it is about dying to self on Earth. Without faith, we cannot move mountains. With faith, we are fearless. We, the children of God, share one gift, the power of the Holy Spirit, which gives us the ability to share the Gospel with the world. He is the wind beneath our wings!

But you will receive power when the Holy Spirit comes on you, and you will be my witnesses... (Acts 1:8)

We are in Him, He is not in us. Therefore, we have all the strength that we need to go forward and transform lives in His name. How beautiful is that?

I wrote this story with love, with the hope that it inspires men and women, who may feel that they lack the ability to grow close to God. We must approach Him with our every request. Going to people for advice is helpful in our Christian walk, because we are one as God's children. Change, however, happens when we go to Him in prayer with our needs—with our total submission. Sometimes we feel He is absent, but that never is the truth, even after we have fouled up. I learned this lesson when I got down on my knees and presented my sins to God and repented. I had been lost. I sought His presence through others, when all that I needed to do was to go to Him with an earnest heart.

If you need God in your life, please go to Him today and ask Him for your forgiveness. Repent from your sins. Ask The Lord to search for and remove any barriers that may be present between you and Him. His grace never fails those that seek and follow Him with commitment.

Then, ask Him to guide your next steps by praying the following prayer:

Heavenly Father, What can I do for You today?

I want You to work through me. I want to witness the transformation of others through You. I am weak without You, Father. Please fill me with Your strength. Please search my heart for obstacles that my keep me from knowing You and Your grace.

I give You the glory! I love You so very much.

In Jesus' Name, Amen.

FROM FEAR TO FREEDOM: HOW LOVE RESCUED ME
By Julene Fleurmond

There was a sea of faces before me. What felt like hundreds of pairs of eyes were staring me down, but they were a blur, because I was too focused on trying to stop the embarrassing trembling of my hands and voice. The pounding of my heartbeat pulsing in my ears and was so loud that I was sure everyone else could hear it as I stood at the podium with my notes quivering in hand.

It felt like I was in a den of lions, with my heart beating furiously and beads of sweat trickling down my face, as I anticipated the felines' ferocious attack. In reality, I was giving a presentation in front of a crowd of about 100 people at my university. I was attempting to describe my passion for empowering youth and discussing a project that I was proposing to create to impact young people in my city. What should have been a 10-minute talk felt like it was lasting forever.

Instead of speaking confidently, I felt insecure and as if I was drowning in the crowd's criticism and rejection before I even could even get my message out. It wasn't that they were jeering with tomatoes in hand ready to pelt me, it was more that I felt inadequate and unworthy to be up there. I thought had nothing important to say.

As a little girl I, was extremely afraid of speaking in front of people. I was so quiet that people would ask my parents if I was mute. I don't remember the first time that I was gripped by fear and anxiety, but it began early on in life. I can trace a significant event at age six when my sister ran away from home. Before she left, she had told my brother and I not to tell our parents. When my parents did find out that she had left, they scolded us, and I felt so ashamed. I thought that I was to blame for her leaving. From that point on, I truly believed that my voice, whether I used it or not, would get me in trouble or bring rejection and disgrace.

When I was asked to share a verse at church, I would burst into tears because I couldn't think of anything to say on the spot. No one, however, knew what was wrong with me. In kindergarten, when I needed to use the restroom, I was too afraid to ask the teacher, and I just painfully held it in. These kinds of incidents continued throughout my childhood and only grew worse as I got older. What my family thought was mere shyness became severe social anxiety, constant panic attacks and bondage by fear.

As a teen I fell into a deep, dark pit of depression and insecurity. I felt extremely lonely and lost passion for life. I stopped doing the activities I had previously enjoyed and once excelled in, like singing, writing and art. When I did use my talents, I performed to please others, and to gain their affection and affirmation. This behavior led me into a cycle of people-pleasing, attempting to find my identity in guys and approval addiction. All of these actions, merged with my fear, left me in a tense, suffocated state of being. I became like a robot going through the motions of life, not realizing that I was sleepwalking.

It was a life-shifting day in my early 20s, when I had an unexpected experience that shook my world. It began after having a complication with my medications caused me to pass out at home. My family took me to the emergency room. Though I don't remember everything that happened around me when I was passed out, I will never forget what God spoke to me and showed me in my spirit. Though I was scared that I might die there in the hospital, the fear didn't last long because an intense feeling of peace, comfort and calm that I'd never felt before embraced me.

It was through a series of intimate visions that He revealed how much He loved me. He showed me that I had a destiny greater than I could imagine. He spoke tenderly to me and asked who told me that I was unworthy and couldn't speak. He told me to stop trying to hold on to my life and circumstances, to stop belittling myself and to trust Him with my heart. He also told me to let go of my own will. He showed me that He controls every beat of my heart. He revealed that He has created each of us wonderfully and He has shown me that He is always there with those of us who believe in Him. I felt His presence in me, like a pulsating energy in my heart that permeated throughout my body, It was shaking me to come awake and align with the rhythm and purpose of Heaven. It was unlike anything that I have ever felt.

During this experience, I had a vision of being in a grand forest, wearing a white dress. Though there wasn't another person in sight, I knew that He was there. God's presence was undeniable. It was a peace and calmness that captured my attention. As I asked Him questions like a curious little girl, He revealed His love for me and for all humanity from the very beginning of time. He shared His plan has always been to redeem us from sin, fear and all that plagues us on this earth. I had never experienced such passion in my life. I never knew so clearly that God existed and had a plan for me, and for all of His children to be part of His grand story of redemption. What He asks in return, as He did in the beginning in the Garden, is our trust, obedience and surrender to His perfect love and will.

This experience has stayed with me since that day, and it has shaped my life and the way that I pursue God and my purpose. I want to seek God deeper as my Father and Beloved, to return to the way it was meant to be in the Beginning, when Adam and Eve walked and communed with Him in close intimacy. I believe this intimacy is also His heart for you. He wants you to seek Him with all of your heart and to allow His love to overcome all of your insecurities because "perfect love casts out fear" (1 John 4:18, ESV). He, in His perfect love, has the best in mind for us as His kids. No matter what our situations look like, He is in control.

Our freedom from fear happened the day that Jesus gave His life for us on the cross and became sin, fear, disease and all that imprisons us. Growing in this freedom has been a day-by-day release of the insecurities that once chained me. I have realized that I am already free and no longer have to hold on to those chains. I can feel Him enveloping me in His liberty and love more and more all the time, as I let go of former limitations and surrender all to Him. He has taught me to let go of anxiety and trying to live in my own strength. I also know that because Jesus is the antidote to my sinful nature, I can have a deep, intimate relationship with God that is beyond anything on Earth. I long to pursue Him in deep, uncommon ways because He is the greatest prize and the fulfillment of every desire that my heart yearns for.

Before I was afraid to speak, to share and to live freely. Now I am freely speaking, sharing and living to show and tell others about the love that saved me. He's given me visions of my destiny—and my passion now is to wake others up from sleepwalking through life so that they realize that they too have significance in Christ. The Enemy prowls around like a lion ready to destroy the gifts and lives of those God holds closely as precious to Him. The very thing that the Enemy attacks in your life is the thing that God wants to use in you to bring others to Him.

Our voices are a powerful force, yet often we relinquish that power. We set aside that force after we're numbed through trials and struggles in life. I believe the Enemy of our souls has a plan to steal and extinguish the power of our voices beginning when we are children. His attacks are especially strong on those who go through abuse and insecurity. Those attacks cause us to neglect the importance and effectiveness of speaking up about what matters. God himself spoke the world into motion in the Beginning with His words. He can breathe His power into us so that we can speak life into the lives of others, reviving them from their spiritual sleepwalking. Darkness tried to snuff out my voice and light at a young age. Now, however, I have found and reclaimed my voice to spread the message and light of the One who saved me.

From speaking engagements to having opportunities to sharing my story in the media, God has been amazing in revealing my purpose and launching me into a brighter hope and a future—and He has the same in store for you. Just last week I stood in front of a group of young people speaking about God's love and purpose for them. Instead of my voice shaking and my heart pounding loudly in my ears, I spoke boldly and my heart beat passionately. That fervor comes because I of my deep desire for others to find freedom in Jesus like I have.

His desire is the same for you as it is for me. He wants you to see beyond the circumstances of your life. He wants you to discover the unwavering, relentless pursuit of a God who so loved you that He gave His only Son up for you. Your future is in the best hands! You can be courageous and boldly reclaim your voice and identity in Him. You can tell your story and be a beacon of light to others, who are waiting to be impacted by the hope you bring through Jesus.

Are you ready to seek the greatest love and live out an extraordinary dream? He's ready to rescue you from darkness, to guide you by His steady, never-ending light and let you know that you are secure in His tender loving arms—forever.

LETTING GOD REINVENT MY PURPOSE
By Cindy Taylor

Think back...way back to 1963. July 30, to be exact. That was the beginning of my journey here on earth! During the past 50ish years, I have learned many things...some lessons were welcomed...some were not. But from every experience came new knowledge and a new perspective. When I look at it that way, I am thankful for each one.

One thing I love to do is listen to people's stories. As a new follower of Christ, I remember listening to testimonies of amazing stories of God's redemption. Many told stories of God's faithfulness through tremendous trials. There always seemed to be a lot of drama! I remember thinking that as a new believer at age 17, I just didn't have that kind of story! I was a responsible teenager who would never think of crossing any lines set out before me. When asked to give MY testimony, I was at a loss. I always felt my story just wasn't dramatic enough!

As the years passed and I grew in my faith, I came to realize that God has a story He is writing about each of our lives. It is the story of faithfulness in the everyday. He is with us each step of the way...if we allow Him in. He sometimes does dramatic things like allowing my mom to die at 55 and leaving me to figure out many things on my own. (The big lesson with this one was to be thankful for those who are still here!). He also provides by allowing exactly the right people to enter our lives at exactly the right time. (There are too many instances of Him teaching me this lesson to even begin to write about them!) He is faithful—that's the bottom line!

So...Here is just a snippet of my journey with God, my faithful companion.

One of my biggest challenges started a few years ago when I had what some might call a midlife crisis. It wasn't the kind of tailspin where I run off to Italy, but rather, it was the kind that I began to ask the big questions. I wondered what was I doing with my life and, more importantly, why was I doing what I was doing? I felt like my life hit a wall—an unexpected roadblock—that I needed to get around, one way or another! I was coming up on 15 years as a consultant with a direct sales book company. I felt that I had taken that business as far as I could, and I needed a change. My family needed less of me as my children were amazing, self-sufficient teenagers and young adults. I needed a new focus. I found myself uninspired. I needed a new challenge!

At the same time, a woman in our church community died suddenly of cancer. To hear about her diagnosis was surprising to all of us. It was hard to reconcile that a woman—who worked with her husband in missions, a mom to six, and friend to many—just shy of 40 years old, would die within days of hearing the word cancer. When I heard the news, God spoke to my spirit, "I have taken her...but YOU are still here...You have more to do." I felt THAT lesson in my gut. My searching began in earnest. *Why AM I still here? What IS my purpose?*

All that I had been pondering bubbled to the surface when I helped my son pack for college in Saskatchewan. We live in Ontario. I remember thinking in my head that this was an amazing opportunity for him to be on his own, learn more about God, music and audio. He was "ready" to go—no doubt about that. My heart, however, was not sure that I was ready for him to go off to school!

A dear friend saw my heavy heart and reached out. She reminded me that I have a single purpose as a parent, and that is to work myself out of a job. My goal was being achieved, and my son was ready. Yea for me! My son leaving for school also made it clear that I need another focus...I needed to find my NEXT purpose!

The problem was, I had NO IDEA what to do next! I spent much time wringing my hands and talking about what I might do. I remember driving to a cottage with my hubby and kids. It was a good five or six-hour trip, and I spent the whole time just throwing out possibilities of a new career direction. To say my family was tired of listening to my career exploration thoughts is an understatement. While it was at the front of my mind, it really wasn't at the front of everyone else's mind...well...except that they wished I would find something to do so I would stop talking about it!

I needed help, so I sought out a coach. To be honest, I wasn't really sure what a coach did, but I had connected with someone online and we set up a call. I was curious. That was the BEST DECISION I could have made! We talked about so many ideas. *What do I value? What am I passionate about? What are my strengths?* She helped me see that there were options, not just roadblocks! It was SO FREEING to see a new road opening up in front of me! After years of nurturing everyone else, it was time to nurture the passions that had been set aside for "someday" that I had buried so deep that I didn't even realize they were present. It was now MY time to step out and do exactly what God wanted me to do next!

And, sometimes life can be surprising when God is in control. I was so taken by the results of talking with my coach that I decided to BECOME a coach! It was like a light turned on inside and I got so excited!! I figured it out...but now what?

I then went into research mode. God lead me to Life Purpose Coaching Centers International and I learned SO MUCH from Kathy, my instructor! I felt that God wanted me to do even more, so I attended the Three-Day Coaching Intensive in Dallas, Texas, with Ultimate Coach University. I was SO BLESSED to be able to learn from Dana and Neil! As I sat in the classroom on day 2, I thought to myself, *This is EXACTLY where God wants me to be.* I LOVED it! I received my certification as a Direct Sales Coach in the fall of 2014. I also took as many webinars as I could fit in my schedule and hope to complete my Life Coaching certification soon!

So, here I am, a certified Life Purpose Coach, a Direct Sales Coach and I even have some specialization in Career Coaching. The next step should be easy peasy, right? I should have clients lined up out the door! And she lived happily ever after, right? Nope...not that simple...but God is faithful, remember? I had many more lessons to learn!

It is one thing to decide to become a coach (or build any kind of business), and it is another to actually earn income being a coach. I didn't know where to begin, so I found a group online that offered a Mastermind Group to help get businesses launched. In this group, we were challenged to narrow our focus and choose a niche. I looked at the options I felt I had: Life Coaching or Direct Sales Coaching. My thinking was that people would not pay for Life Coaching as much as people would pay for Direct Sales coaching. My reasoning was that Direct Sales people were wanting to make money, so they would invest in someone to help them be more successful. In theory, I was right...in practice...not so much. Looking back, I made a fatal error. I talked to others and made assumptions, but I did not talk to God about my decision. And there began months of spinning wheels, desperately trying to get traction on a business that God had not directed me to! Is God faithful even when we don't make a wise choice? YES! Is God faithful allowing us to go down a winding road, filled with lessons along the way? Also YES! I will say that there was much time, and even more money, spent on that winding road...but I wouldn't trade it for anything!

Here are some lessons I learned along the way...

1. **God is Faithful.** This bears repeating. Even with unwise (dare I say, self-directed) choices, God has kept us afloat economically! He has made the way for us to maintain a roof over our head and food on the table. He has been with us and continues to be with us, every step of the journey.

2. **God loves me.** God wants the best for His children. He has surrounded me with people that love me and support me, even when I go off on bunny trails. He can't love me any more and He can't love me any less than He already does. That's because His love is not based on anything I have done...His love is unconditional.

3. **God wants us to learn.** Life is filled with what we perceive as failures. Does God see these experiences this way? I wonder if He just sees them as opportunities for us to learn and do something different the next time. I think WE often seem them just as failures. I want to see all experiences as God sees them!

4. **God gives us options.** The amazing thing about how God operates is that He allows us choices....good or bad. We can choose to run our business (and our

lives) by walking with God or we can choose to give it a try on our own. Based on the last 3 years of my life, I now choose to do it in partnership with God. And what has been the biggest lesson of all? Talk to God about EVERYTHING! It can't get any simpler than that!

How did it all work out? Well...it isn't over yet. Where I am at the moment is talking to God more...and He is working WITH me to move me in a different direction. As soon as I talked it over with Him, He sent me on a different path, one that stirs me up inside...not one that stresses me! Each day of TRYING to build a business in my own strength was stressful and just plain hard. It is amazing the peace that I have felt since deciding to shift directions! I am so thankful ...

And what happened when I started to talk to God on a regular basis about my new path? He started bringing along EXACTLY the right people and exactly the right resources at exactly the right time. And the peace continues...and the amazement at God's faithfulness continues!

And this is what I DO know! It has been a THRILL to come alongside others, women just like me (and perhaps you), that want more, and to help them find their own unique path! I LOVE walking the journey with people just like you. How much easier is it to walk the journey with someone who has "been there, done that!" I have shed my share of tears along the way. It is with this kind of knowing heart—as one who has walked this journey—that I can listen with knowing ears. I can hear YOUR heart and the hearts of so many other women just like us. I know what it is that I most appreciated about my friend who came alongside me. I really just wanted someone to hear me and to understand me. The Lord made me (and you) and He totally understands me (and you). In this understanding, He shows his faithfulness. THIS I know for sure!

WHEN GOD CALLS, IT'S NEVER A WRONG NUMBER
By Patricia "Pat" Sabiston

During my tenure as an elected official, many people would come up to me and say: "I just couldn't do what you're doing." My response?

"Well, of course you could—*if* God *asked* you to do it."

It always bothered me when Christians would say, "No, no, I *really* couldn't do it."

I didn't think I could enter politics either, but God never leaves us or forsakes us. And even though politics is often a nasty, dirty business, if God calls you to it, it becomes a matter of obedience. More importantly, I can tell you this: our cities, states and nation are in dire need of Christians who are brave enough to enter these arenas of personal service and sacrifice, paying what I term their "civic collateral."

My walk with Christ began at a Billy Graham Crusade when I was nine years old, but it wasn't until May 2001, when I took Henry Blackaby's *Experiencing God* study, that I finally understood what having a *personal* relationship with Jesus Christ entailed. It was the *ultimate* ah-ha moment!

During the course of my study, I gave God my life to do with as He pleased. I truly meant it, or at least I *thought* I did, until "The Call" came.

Surely, SURELY God wasn't asking me to do what I thought He was asking. Politics? I've always *hated* politics ever since I witnessed the "dirty side" of it through my mother's involvement as a party chairperson in my hometown. Bomb threats at dinner weren't unusual.

Since that time, I've learned that God has a wonderful sense of humor, so when I responded to his initial "Call" with: "Couldn't you just send me to the mission field in Africa instead?" His answer was patient and kind, but firm. "I said I want you to run for your local school board."

Now, understand, I've had many communications with God before, but only a very few times have I heard His audible voice. In my heart, I *knew* this was Him, but I still had doubts, so I made an appointment with my pastor to confirm what I was hearing.

"When you get a Call, how do you know it's real?" I asked. "How do you know it is God and not your subconscious?"

My pastor was as patient and kind as God had been, but then that's in his job description. "It's very simple, just ask Him and He'll tell you," he explained.

Since I *really* didn't *want* to do what God asked, rather than doing what this man of God suggested, I sought *other* counsel from the community's Republican leadership, my party of choice. Even though the race would be non-partisan, I still would need help from people I knew well. The meeting resulted in *just* the outcome I desired.

"Pat, there is absolutely no way you can win the School Board election," my friend said with exasperation. "First, your opponent is the incumbent. Second, he's male and you aren't." He smiled at the obvious. "Third, he goes to the biggest Baptist church in the city. Fourth, he's got 12 years of experience behind him, and you have none. Fifth, he's a 'local,' and you 'ain't from here'. Sixth, he's an independent business owner with lots of deep roots into the community. Seventh ..." I raised my hand to stop him, having heard enough, but he added: "So if you want to stick your toe into the political pool, just to see what it's like, dive in, but don't be disappointed in the outcome."

I was elated! I was *certain* when the Lord heard what came from the Republican's mouth to His ears he'd *surely* tell me He wasn't serious about his request.

That night, I very confidently knelt and began—"Well, Lord, I know you're aware of my meeting today, so I'm sorry that I can't answer your 'Call.' What *else* do you have for me to do?"

God became even more persistent. "I am God. You told me you believe I am who I say I am. I have asked you to do something very specific, and I'm expecting you to be obedient."

"But what if I run and lose?" The thought of a very public embarrassment in a very small town, along with being labeled a "loser," was nauseating. (There was that "pride" thing rearing its ugly head.) I remained silent, anxiously awaiting His response.

"I want you to totally trust me, *regardless* of the outcome. Plus, this isn't about you."

Experiencing God author Blackaby had said to expect this crisis of faith, but I guess I had forgotten that part of the study.

So, I stepped out in faith, walking on very shaky feet, into an uncertain future.

Before I announced my candidacy for the board position, wise counsel from many Christian friends told me I should advise my opponent *before* he heard it "on the street" or in the media.

He and I met at the school board's administrative offices, and to say that this 12-year incumbent was surprised by my pending announcement was an understatement. When he asked why I was running, I told him about The Call, to which he responded—"Well, I don't feel 'called' to step down." So he and I agreed that we would each run a clean, non-confrontational race, and that's exactly what we did. As a matter of fact, our county's Supervisor of Elections *still* holds our race up as the "ideal" manner in which to run a potentially contentious campaign. And it was God who provided me instructions in this area of need as well!

As I sat at my computer, wondering what to put on the Supervisor of Election's mandatory website, I remembered a recent comment from a male peer. "This ain't gonna be a 'beauty contest' Sabiston. You need to come out swinging!"

This statement disturbed me because I've never considered myself to be an aggressive, political animal. So I bowed my head over my keyboard and asked God for guidance. He directed me to Titus 2. As I began to read this text that serves as a mentoring lesson, I thought, *Lord, what does older women training the young women have to do with my website content?* But I kept reading until this text jumped off the page:

> *"In everything set them an example by doing what is good. In your teaching show integrity, seriousness and soundness of speech that cannot be condemned, so that those who oppose you may be ashamed because they have nothing bad to say about us"* (Titus 2:7–8, NIV).

So those verses became my campaign's marching orders, and I kept them in mind during the next several months of trying to convince voters I should be their choice for the position.

A well-known verse from Proverbs reminds us to *"Trust in the Lord with all your heart, and lean not on your own understanding. In all your ways acknowledge Him, and He shall direct your paths"* (Proverbs 3:5, AKJV).

Opportunities to speak came, seemingly, "out of nowhere." But right in the middle of the race, I fell down some uneven stairs and had to wear a boot cast, which precluded me from being able to walk neighborhoods to, personally, meet voters, so I literally "rested" on Proverbs 3:5.

On the night of the election, my race broke all local history records! I won, but by just one ... ONE (1) ... vote, out of more than 45,000 ballots cast! My husband grinned broadly and said, "Isn't this *just* like God?" A landslide wouldn't have been nearly as dramatic, and to God be the glory. Of course, it was understood that with such a close race, a recount would be necessary and mandatory.

During the detailed recount process, candidates are required to be on site at the local Supervisor of Elections' office to watch, and validate, the painstaking process. While I was there, I spent the time crocheting, because just like before, I didn't *want* to do what was being asked of me by God, so I was *extremely* relaxed. My opponent sat and watched every move and decision of the Canvassing Board, making notes on a small scratch pad. As the numbers that separated us dwindled, my opponent asked me—"Pat, if both of us felt 'called,' and I lose, what is the lesson for me?"

I said, "I don't know." But remembering my pastor's previous counsel, I added, "Why don't you ask God? He'll tell you."

A holiday separated the first two days of the recount from the last, so as we regrouped to spend just one additional, tiresome day together, my opponent said, "Well, I received my answer." I looked at him, wondering if he were going to share his revelation, when he continued.

"In all the years of our marriage, my wife and I have always discussed and prayed over major decisions." He paused and took a deep breath. "But, as we were driving to a brief vacation over the weekend, my wife reminded me that this was the first time, ever, that I made a decision and left her out of the process."

I thought, *God is always so very literal in answering our prayers, if we will only ask Him.*

When the final count went from one victory point on the night of the election, to just two votes in my favor after the three-day count, an official announcement was made before the media. I reached over and hugged my brother in Christ. The media seemed to find this action to be a bit unusual to say the least, as it was posted on the front page of the newspaper the following day.

The Supervisor of Elections was most relieved that we accepted the final results of the recount marathon, since Florida had been part of the "hanging chad" fiasco just recently. I was also in a state of shock, concerned about what lay before me, but was most proud of the road that my Lord and I had traveled to this point. And, we gave the media—and the community—something to talk about that they *still* do to this day, *especially* when someone says their vote doesn't count! But I always try to bring people back to the center of it all—God's Call and the necessity to always find out where He is working, and then join Him there.

I served, I believe, very honorably for four years. Being in politics had many high points, but also many low points. One night in particular, at the end of a particularly difficult session, I was lying in bed crying and calling out to God.

"Lord, you called me to this political seat, but this is horrible! People are so mean and hateful! Do you know how horrible politics is?"

Almost immediately the response came: "Don't forget, it was politics that killed my Son."

I felt so ashamed of my whining, and tried to keep my complaints to Him at a minimum from that point on.

During my years of service, there were so many stories of His guidance; they seemed to come in like daily heavenly telegraphs.

So, I want to encourage you to immediately "pick up" on "The Call" when you receive it. Remember: God usually chooses very ordinary people to accomplish extraordinary things, but the most important question is: *What are you risking if you don't answer that Call?*

Even though I'm no longer in politics, God's Word is alive and active in my life, and I know He wants to be in yours, but … it's a matter of obedience.

Beauty For Ashes Press

LISTENING TO GOD'S LIFE-GIVING WORDS

Beauty For Ashes Press

DECEIVED NO MORE
By Elin Criswell

On Saturday, October 19, 1998, I prayed with my husband. I told God that I finally, finally, really understood. I acknowledged that I was a sinner. I thanked Jesus for dying on the cross for me, I placed my faith in Him and accepted His free gift of salvation. I told God that I loved Him and I opened my eyes, redeemed. Later when I told others, they were *surprised*. You see, for 37 years I had lived my life as a Christian, when I was not. The thing is, I thought I was a Christian.

When I was six years old, I prayed the sinner's prayer. In my mind, I can still picture this event. I had gone to church that morning feeling guilty. I had had some disagreement with my mom, over what, I can't remember. But I knew I was wrong and I felt guilty. My Sunday School teacher gave the lesson, and as she did often, while we were all bowed in prayer, she asked if anyone wanted to pray the sinner's prayer. I raised my hand. I prayed. I thought I became a Christian. Life went on.

By the time I was a teenager, although I was very much considered one of those *good girls*, I went through my own phase of rebellion. It got to the point where I knew I was headed down the wrong road, and I made the decision that I simply didn't want to go there. So I repented. I rededicated my life to Christ and was baptized. I wanted the world to know that I meant business with God. Little did I know, I still wasn't saved.

Years later, when I graduated from high school, I didn't know what I wanted to do with my life. I came from a family of humble means. College wasn't an option, nor did I really care to go. I had few interests, but I finally fell back on the skills that I did have. I found a job as a secretary. I held that job for a year, but then I learned about a Bible school that a friend of mine was attending. This opportunity piqued my interest, so off I went on a day trip to visit my friend and the school. I came home with the strong desire to attend that school.

At the time, that Bible school was unaccredited. They offered a year-long program of in-depth study of the Word of God. I absolutely loved my time in that beautiful part of the country in 1981, and I made a lot of friends, but going to Bible school didn't save me either.

Once again I reached an end, and I didn't know what to do with my life. I had thought strongly about going to the Philippians as a missionary, but the funds weren't there. What should I do? I went home to good ol' mom and dad.

Now I had grown up in Austin, Texas, but the year before I went to Bible school my parents had moved twenty five miles north to the country. I now needed to acclimate to a new area. I also wanted to find work locally instead of commuting to Austin. In the process, I also ended up finding a new church.

I had grown up attending the Evangelical Free Church, a good, Bible teaching church that taught the truth about Jesus. During my high school years, I became very involved with youth group activities both at our local church and on a state wide basis. Leadership qualities within me surfaced. But being involved and doing good works didn't save me either. As the old saying goes, *"Standing in the garage doesn't make you a car —just like going to church doesn't make you a Christian."*

God directed me to a new church home, at a Baptist Church. Meeting the new pastor was a shock. I have joked many times that growing up, I thought all pastors were born in three-piece suits, but that pastor threw me for a loop because he was a much more casual sort of man. When people would visit him and his family at home, they would most likely find him wearing jeans or shorts, a t-shirt and flip flops. One of his favorite activities was to be outside tending his plants. As he did that, he prayed. My pastor and his wife made Christianity *real* for me.

The years went on and life was good. I met my husband-to-be, Danny, in church. We fell in love and were married in July 1986. The birth of our children came in the years that followed. But as time went on, life just seemed to get more and more frustrating. It seemed that I didn't have the inner strength to face life's challenges, and the longer you live, the more challenges you face.

Our beloved pastor died in June 1993. Two years later, my mom died of cancer. These were two very devastating blows. Then came the day when my elderly dad fell and broke his leg. Our lives totally changed when we became his primary caregivers, but God knew exactly what He was doing.

Dealing with my dad on a 24/7 basis, brought me face to face with deeply buried issues in my life that had been long forgotten. My dad was my first image, so to speak, of God the Father. The problem is, growing up I had big issues with Dad. He deeply hurt my heart over and over again with all his broken promises—but unfulfilled promises were not the real issue. The real problem was that I longed to feel loved by my dad. Instead, I felt like he always kept me at arm's length. He was always distant, and as a result, I felt rejected. Unknowingly, I had transferred this feeling of rejection to

God. For many years, I never really believed that God loved me; as a result, I had always held God at arm's length.

God used my husband to show me this connection. Danny had always been a great example to me, showing me consistent love. That October morning as we talked all this over, he looked at me and said, *"God is NOT your daddy."* That statement was what it took. The scales fell from my eyes and for the first time I could see, I could understand. Yes, God really loves *me*. We prayed, and I entered into my relationship with Christ.

I had prayed the sinner's prayer as a child, but reciting mere words mean nothing when no real belief is behind those words. I had never placed my faith in Christ because deep down I had never believed that God really loved me. I do not believe that my experience is rare (see Matthew 7:21–23). But this much I know, if you truly desire to know Jesus, you will. He will show you the Truth, and He will show you what is holding you back. He will not allow you to stay deceived!

As life went on, things sure were different! Now I actually had God's grace to live. In actually knowing the Lord, I could now put to use all the principles I had been taught from the Bible. Instead of going through the motions of living the Christian life, I was actually living it. Over time, I also came to understand that my daddy did love me. My parents really had tried the best they could.

I think that we all tend to have our *daddy* stories, *somebody did me wrong stories*, even, *that church did me wrong* stories. But in the end, it all comes down to you and your decision for or against Christ. When you stand before Him in Heaven, no one else will be to blame.

As long as people are breathing, they have hope. I really believe that God gives each and every person every opportunity to receive His free gift of salvation. If you really want to know Him, He won't allow you to stay deceived. His love will break through.

Beauty For Ashes Press

DRAW NEAR
By Katie Clifton

"No, in all these things we are more than conquerors through him who LOVED (author's emphasis) us. For I am sure that neither death nor life, nor angels nor rulers, nor things present nor things to come, nor powers, nor height nor depth, nor anything else in all creation, will be able to separate us from the LOVE (author's emphasis) of God in Christ Jesus our Lord" (Romans 8:37–39, ESV).

God speaks to me. Sometimes it's in the mundane, ordinary pace of life. Sometimes it is on the mountaintops, and other times I hear Him as I am walking through a valley. Typically the Lord speaks to me through scripture, prayer, a song, the wise words of a faithful follower…rarely has it been an audible voice. God chooses to communicate with us because of the incomprehensible love He has for us.

On January 2, 2013, as I slept, I had a dream and I heard from the Lord. In my dream, Jared (my husband) and I were in a dark room with no light, but we were able to see each other in the darkness. We were holding hands and standing side by side. Our backs were being pressed against the wall behind us with what felt like the gravitational force of a roller coaster. In front of us was a thick heavy fog. This supernatural darkness was bearing down against us though it wasn't tangible. We were terrified. Jared and I never spoke to one another, but it was as if we knew what the other felt. Neither of us knew how to cry out or what to say for our rescue. As the darkness pressed harder, we heard the Lord say, "Draw near." He spoke three times before Jared and I began to say these words with the Lord. Each time I let those words come out, I felt more freedom from the weight of the darkness. I could breathe a bit deeper with each word that escaped my mouth. I began to get louder each time, until I yelled, "Draw near!"

Jared woke me up because I was yelling in my sleep. I woke up, knowing I was meant to pray for someone. I was completely unsure whom the Lord was leading me to pray for. When morning came, I couldn't shake my dream. As I reflected back over the details and unspoken emotions in the darkness, Jared urged me to look up every scripture about drawing near. As I continued through my ordinary routine of getting ready, I was reading a verse I have on my bathroom mirror: *"Put on the full armor of God, so that you can take your stand against the devil's schemes. For our struggle is not against flesh and blood, but against the rulers, against the authorities, against the powers of this dark world and against the spiritual forces of evil in the heavenly realms"* (Ephesians 6:11–12, NIV). As I read that verse I opened my You Version Bible app and God led me directly to a verse in Proverbs: *"Trust in the Lord with all your heart and lean not on your own understanding; in all your ways submit to him, and he will make your paths straight"* (Proverbs 3:5–6, NIV). When I read that verse, God told me who I was to specifically pray for: my sister. I immediately texted her to share that God had told me to pray that verse over her that day. I prayed hard for her. I examined that passage and tried to understand what God was telling me, yet ironically, I leaned on my own understanding.

I could not shake God's command to draw near. My heart was so heavy that I couldn't forget the words. As I went through the ordinary routine of my workday, I paused at work to look up verses as my husband had urged me to look up. One of them was Psalm 145:18–19, NIV, which says: *"The*

Lord is near to all who call on him, to all who call on him in truth. He fulfills the desires of those who fear him...he hears their cry and saves them." Another one was James 4:8, NIV, which says: *"Draw near to God, and he will draw near to you. Cleanse your hands, you sinners, and purify your hearts, you double-minded."*

Within an hour of reading and writing down these verses, I received a phone call from my mom. The news was tragic. My sister's husband had shot himself. This kind of news shakes your soul and spins your comprehension of life upside down all in a single moment. I hung up, left work in a state of shock and drove to their home, praying God would use me to help by brother in law. As I arrived policemen and firemen met me. I was shaking uncontrollably, heart broken at the situation, sick and unable to wrap my mind around the reality before me. I watched as a helicopter landed to transport him to the hospital. The detectives were hopeful he would survive, but they said it was "bad."

Within minutes, I was faced with an overwhelming darkness. The scene of His suicide was shown to us by the police. We chose that moment as an opportunity to serve my sister. What our eyes saw, our minds could not fully comprehend. The scene was horrific. Haunting. Heart breaking. We were surrounded by darkness. We could feel the warfare that had taken place inside their home that morning. In that moment of physical, mental and emotional paralysis, I wasn't even sure what to pray or how to pray. I began saying out loud, *"I can do all things through Christ who gives me strength!"* (Philippians 4:13, NIV). That verse was all I could think of. I said it over and over as I cried and shook and yelled out to God for help. I was saying it so that I would believe it.

We needed God to strengthen us and we needed Satan to hear God's Word so that he would leave. Then God said to me," Draw near." In that moment of the most intense darkness I have ever experienced, my back was pressed against a spiritual wall. I was being pressed down by the darkness. It was heavy and overwhelming. I remembered *"Our battle is not against the flesh but with the evil in this world"* (Ephesians 6:11, HCSB).I looked at my husband and knew in my spirit that this moment was the one God had spoken to me about.

As God told me again to "Draw near," He was giving me a peace that He had gone before us. He is always going before us. God is so faithful! He is agape love! He is omnipotent, omnipresent, the Alpha and the Omega! The storm that began that day has not passed...yet. But God is working in this storm. He is showing us daily to not lean on our own understanding, but in all our ways acknowledge Him and He will lower the mountains, lift the valleys and make our paths straight. The Lord is worthy to be trusted.

God has something greater for us. There IS something greater for us all. Sometimes the greater comes in the ordinary. Sometimes He reveals His plans on the mountaintop and sometimes He calls us to greater as we walk with Him through the valley. Greater is He that is in us than he that is in the world. This world is fallen. This world is not our home. This world surrounds us with sorrows. Sometimes the darkness presses us against a wall: fearful, unsure of what to pray and unaware of our escape.

"Draw near." These two words have become a promise from my Savior—they are His words of love for me. These words give me a peace that surpasses all understanding. These words breathe hope into despair. They shine light into the darkness. They set the captive free. They give comfort when our hearts are broken. God never changes! He spoke to numerous people throughout Scripture and He still speaks to us. His desire is to be heard. We—you and I—need to know Him more. But, we do not need more of God—He needs more of us.

Sometimes God speaks to me. Sometimes (more often) my heart is so cluttered with idols and sin that I don't allow my ears to hear His voice. Sometimes God speaks on the mountain. Sometimes He talks in the valley. But find comfort and rest in that whatever circumstances you face. He has gone before you. God, in His infinite LOVE for us has chosen to go before us, the sinful, the shameful, the disobedient, the unworthy.

Deuteronomy 31:6, 8, ESV, says: *"Be strong and courageous. Do not fear or be in dread of them, for it is the Lord your God who goes with you. He will not leave you or forsake you... It is the Lord who goes before you. He will be with you; he will not leave you or forsake you. Do not fear or be dismayed."* He promises again to us in Deuteronomy 1:30-31, ESV: *"The Lord your God who goes before you will himself fight for you, just as he did for you in Egypt before your eyes, and in the wilderness, where you have seen how the Lord your God carried you, as a man carries his son, all the way that you went until you came to this place"*.

"For this light momentary affliction is preparing for us an eternal weight of glory beyond all comparison, as we look not to the things that are seen but to the things that are unseen. For the things that are seen are transient, but the things that are unseen are eternal" (2 Corinthians 4:17–18,

ESV). God is so great! He is worthy of our praise. He is worthy to be trusted. His unfailing LOVE never runs out. The Lord takes ashes and brings beauty. He takes our pain and delivers healing. He sees our brokenness and begins restoration. He gives us a way out. When there seems to be no way, He makes the way.

My mind often still fixes on the horrible sights of that day. Yet here I am—two years later—and I'm standing on the other side of the valley. The Lord was so good, so gracious, to allow me in that situation. I walk through seasons where I ache to feel that closeness with Him again—to hear His voice. When we are brought to our knees, when the carpet has been ripped out from under out feet, there is freedom in the fall...because we can trust The One who catches us.

FROM CHICAGO BLUES TO TENNESSEE BLUEBIRDS
By Loral Robben Pepoon

It was a frigid January Saturday afternoon in Chicago. I was lying in bed, exhausted with swollen eyes from crying all day. I was wrecked over shattered dreams and unfulfilled expectations as I reflected on my life. I was 40 years old, single and living in a tiny room, located in a bad neighborhood with another struggling woman and her barking, peeing dog. Normally, I would exercise or go do something to fight these battles with overwhelming sorrow. Today, however, I was snowed in and frigid to the bone on a sub-zero degree day—getting out from under the blankets wasn't going to happen. Just as I thought I couldn't sink any lower into my depressive pit, the phone rang.

One of my best friends who had been a rock to me through the last decade called. She told me that she was engaged. I pretended to be thrilled for her, but a knife went through my heart. This stab was deep because it reminded me of my poor choices. I was thrilled for her, but I was also kicking myself because she was marrying someone who had asked me out a couple years earlier—and I had said no. At the time, I was stuck in a non-committed, dysfunctional, long distance relationship.

More than two years later, that non-committing man still hadn't committed to me or shown any signs of holding a stable job. Yet, I was still wasting hours talking—OK mostly fighting—on the phone. We blamed each other for our broken personal lives that were not moving forward.

I know this relationship's drain on me contributed to the decline of prosperity in all areas of my life. It certainly didn't help me cope with an overly demanding job. If I earned enough money to live on my own in this world-class city, I would have accepted the extra 10–20 hours a week as part of the sacrifice. However, four years earlier, when I wanted to live more and work less, I accepted a different job with a 25% pay cut because I was told that it rarely required extra hours—that was not the case.

 With less income, I had to move in with roommates to pay the bills. The first roommate situation was wonderful, but she got engaged. Her condo sold more quickly than expected and I had a couple of weeks to find a new place to live. With extra hours at work, I didn't have time to apartment shop. I moved in with an acquaintance and was thankful to have a roof over my head—albeit in an unsafe area with the company of a barking, peeing dog.

The same month that I had to move, I also learned that my boss took away half of my responsibilities and restructured my job. Although the reduction of duties was welcome, I no longer got to be responsible for the half of my job that functioned well and provided creative nourishment. I was left with the half that was overtaxing.

In addition, for three years, I couldn't muster up enough energy to function optimally for the entire day. I had brain fog, frequent headaches and was tired—no matter how much I slept. My doctor had told me during several visits that I was too stressed and that I needed another job. Well, I had tried that, and my health and energy hadn't changed. I couldn't shake the feeling that something was wrong. I finally found an integrative medicine doctor who really listened to me. We found out that I was anemic and severely Vitamin D deficient. Praise God that we had gotten to the root of my exhaustion! I began to take supplements and eat intentionally to fix the problems. It took me a couple years to get my vitamin levels back to normal.

In the meantime however, with a disappointing job reassignment, a counterfeit phone relationship, a vitamin-deficient body and a challenging living situation, I was miserable. I would find myself crying out to God more than ever. I had been a Christian for more than a decade, but I was stuck in a cycle of constantly working harder—and even at a ministry—to atone for my sin and shortcomings. I thought I could earn God's favor by doing His work professionally, even though I was still not consistently seeking him.

God never stopped wooing me to Himself. I would have periodic amazing moments and weekends away filled with peace. Once every few months, I would visit a dear friend who lived on the Maumee River in Ohio. We would seek God together on a special swing, situated on the Maumee's banks. We created spiritual retreats, and we cried out to God to change and redeem our lives from the muck of the past and the present. These moments and close feelings to God would fade as I put God in the back seat behind life's daily grind.

I soon learned, however, that when God wants to get your attention to change your life, He doesn't stay in that back seat. Instead, He may allow all of your circumstances to deteriorate so that you notice Him all the time. When everything is failing, you have to seek Him more than in just the "time outs" of life. In those moments, when we are barely hanging on, we learn—as I did— that we have to keep holding on to Jesus for dear life.

That phone call about my friend's engagement, on that frigid January day, was one of those moments when He got my attention. I realized that I was only hanging on to life by a thread. After I hung up, I grabbed and climbed my lifeline rope with everything I had. I came out of my room, puffy eyed and red from sobbing, and told the woman I lived with that I needed help. I needed prayer—right then! We prayed, and I resolved to allow God to change my life—all of it—and to not be scared of the unknown. I would do whatever He said.

The first instruction I heard was for me to go ahead and attend a writing/platform building conference in Nashville that I had been considering. It was a way I could love myself on Valentine's Day, instead of lamenting over my singleness. I plunked down the cash for the conference and bought the airline ticket.

I had taken a first step!

I also believed that it was not a coincidence that this conference started the day after a spiritual retreat that I would be attending in Colorado. I fully expected that God would speak to me at the retreat, and that he would steer the course of my life into a new direction—soon.

I also knew that I needed a dear friend to walk through this time with me before the retreat and conference I had always wanted to study *Breaking Free*, by Beth Moore. I called one of my best friends and we started a group study together. I committed to more consistent Bible study and writing.

As I was abiding in Jesus Christ daily, I realized that He had always been available to set me free. I had not always I believed His freedom was for me. As I sat at God's feet, I began to internalize that His offer of joy was not only for someday in Heaven—or just available in moments on earth—but that it was available to me on an everyday basis—both to help me get through trials and to have an abundant life on earth.

A few weeks later at the Colorado retreat just before the Nashville conference, the retreat leader asked me, "When are you moving to Nashville?" I was surprised because I had told him I was going to a conference there, but not that I was thinking of moving there. It was one of the places that I thought I could live *someday*, but I had other places in mind, too.

As the weekend progressed, however, I was convinced that I was supposed to be looking for signs from God to confirm a move to Nashville. I trusted this leader, knowing that he hears from God. Most importantly, I knew and expected that Jesus would speak to me with signs and show me His love and plans. He did just that when we did a group exercise where we share the verses that God had us studying, and then we ask Him to speak to us through words and images.

The verses I had been focusing on were part of the *Breaking Free* study.

"Rise up, my love, my fair one, and come away. For lo, the winter is past, the rain is over and gone, the flowers appear on the earth. The time of singing has come. And the voice of the turtledove is heard in our land...Let me hear your voice;

For your voice is sweet" (Song of Solomon 2:5–10, 14, NKJV).

And: *"Come and hear, all you who fear God, and I will declare what He has done for my soul"* (Psalm 66:16, NKJV).

When I studied these verses, I saw that they were active. I had to come to God, and that He was bringing me into a new season. And, He wants to hear my voice! Because He finds my voice sweet, I am able to share what He has done for my soul.

The words I received both from myself and the others praying with me were: "bluebirds," "blueberries," "rocking chair," "coffee in the morning," and "joy and light coming in."

I also wrote down: *Freedom, symbolized by the birds, comes before the fruit. And that I have to sit in the morning to be warmed and filled up.*

I had no idea what these words and this sentence meant for me. I just knew to begin looking for confirmation of these words in Nashville.

The next day, at the Nashville conference, a woman started praying in the lobby with her hands up for me. She asked that God would make it very clear that I was supposed to move permanently. This conference was not a faith-based conference, but she certainly believed in the power of prayer and wasn't ashamed of it!

The fulfillments of the words I had received started immediately. I went to the bathroom at the conference, and the liquid soap had both the word "blueberries" and a picture of blueberries on the bottle.

Then, in the break between lunch and dinner, I went to a small town nearby, not knowing that the shops would be closed so early. One shop was still open, where I saw a small dish with a bluebird and a blue bird key chain. Both items were under five dollars, so I bought them.

I was staying with my former neighbor from Chicago who now rented a room in a lovely home situated on five acres. The next morning, I sat in a chair that rocked, had my coffee and the sun was coming in from the East, warming me, just as the image and words I had seen. I sat my coffee down on the table, and saw both *bluebirds and blueberries* on coasters. I also had noticed a sugar bowl that had a bluebird on the top of it.

Later that week, a real bluebird was flying across the window of my car, in slow motion like you see in the movies. It was so close to my car, that I should have hit the bird, but I didn't.

That Sunday, the church I visited had a CD for sale, *Songs of Freedom*, with a large bluebird on the cover.

These signs, along with the beauty and peace I felt there were enough to show me that if I didn't move, I would always wonder what I had missed.

Even though I knew I was going to move, I kept asking God to confirm the decision. I was going to be visiting with three dear friends in the coming months and wanted to pray about the move with them.

First, I went to see my friend in California. As she prepared for my visit, she had received additional groceries in her bag by mistake. She called the store to tell them about it, and they said just to keep the items. These items were ALL blueberry flavored items…snacks, yogurt, etc. As we prayed together, she was in agreement that I should move.

The next weekend, I went to visit the friend I mentioned earlier, who lived on the Maumee River in Ohio. Because our prayers also confirmed that I was to move, I called the woman who owned the Tennessee home, where I had stayed a few weeks earlier for the conference. I asked her if I could rent the room permanently. She said that she hadn't been looking for another renter, but she felt I was supposed to move in. So, I was invited to move into the place where I had first seen the signs fulfilled with bluebirds, blueberries, the rocking chair, and the sun shining in the morning.

A couple weeks later, I visited my third friend, who lived in Florida. Much prayer with her also confirmed the move to Nashville. The coolest confirmation was on the trip home. I was praying on the plane, because the next day I was going to give my notice at work—I was about to cut off my livelihood! I had to stop and change planes in Nashville. I was walking through the airport, thinking how much nicer and spacious the Nashville airport is with music playing and cool shops than the body-bumping experience at Chicago Midway. Just then, I received a text from my dear friend who lived in the home where I had stayed during my recent visit to Tennessee. The text said, *"A bluebird is sitting on the tree outside your bedroom window!"*

That was it! I had prayed for another sign and God had given it. I prayed and felt sure that it was time to move forward with my plan to move.

When I told my boss about my plans, she was skeptical, yet supportive. Despite my struggles there, after I left the company, my boss offered me freelance work. That income helped me well into my first year in Tennessee.

As I was driving into Nashville to start my new life, I will never forget the feeling as I saw the rolling green hills, the beautiful homes and the spring flower blooms. I knew that I was finally at peace. I remembered the words of the verse about the winter being over, and the flowers appearing on the earth.

Five generations ago, my ancestors lived in Tennessee. My grandma always talked about how her relatives missed the trees and Tennessee's rolling hills after they relocated to Kansas. I know that beauty here ministers to me each day.

Since I moved to Tennessee, I have taken time each day to abide in Christ each morning. I read, pray, write and ask for Him to continue to show me more signs and visions.

He has given me so many additional signs with bluebirds and blueberries—along with other "God kisses" and lessons from things I love in creation like cats, snails, shells, turtles, deer and butterflies. If I wrote those lessons here, they would take up this entire book. But, I did write them all down in my rocking chair, as the light came in, as was prophesied, and someday I will publish those stories as well.

But, I can share some patterns here: First, I consistently saw one blue bird when God was revealing His love to deeply heal my heart when I first moved. Then, He continued to speak to me about being fruitful and healthy. My body returned to complete health and I lost more than 20 pounds. In a peaceful nourishing environments, I eventually was able to cut the chord with my former boyfriend.

Jesus also reinforced the words in Song of Solomon that He had given me about my voice being sweet. Out of obedience, I began sharing my testimony with groups. One time I even shared it at a women's conference with more than 500 ladies. As I was sharing what He has done for my soul, I began to see two bluebirds together on a regular basis. Then, my friends witnessed the sign of two birds with me one day at church. A few days later, I met the man who would become my husband.

Our dating story and engagement was sweeter than I could have imagined, complete with many blueberries consumed, bluebird sightings and other confirmation words from God. When we were dating, we went to my dear friend's wedding in Ohio. While we were there, we went to that special swing on the Maumee River, where I had been praying for my future husband for years and asking God about my move to Tennessee. After the wedding, my husband even asked me to marry him on that swing!

God won many spiritual battles through struggling prayers on that swing. He also demonstrated His love for me by allowing some of the happiest moments of my life to unfold there. Recently, my husband and I went back to sit on that swing. I was overcome with emotion as I realized how God has changed my life—at that place and wherever I was—all by allowing me to hear His Words and by Him answering my prayers.

Today, my husband and I spend about an hour listening, praying and being with God each morning. Jesus continues to guide us through words, images, and specific instructions. Our job is just to listen and follow.

We are loving our life, flying free together, abiding in Christ, wherever He directs—just like the two bluebirds I saw with friends years ago.

Beauty For Ashes Press

IDENTITY CRISIS
By Alicia Terry

God, who do you say I am? That's the question I should have been asking myself nearly 15 years ago. It's taken me this long to realize that asking the "who" question is about my relationship with God (who I am in Him) and asking the "what" questions, like: *What is my purpose? What am I here to do?"* are about performance. These are great questions—necessary questions, in fact. However, putting them before the *who* question can lead to a pursuit of the project and not the Promiser.

How often do we think about *what* we can do for God instead of about *who* we are in Him? I dare say it's easier to wrap our minds around doing something simply because it is tangible. We can plan it and put action to it. But when it comes to *who* we are in Him, that is a different story that we can't put into action as easily. That's because it's a story that requires faith. Our flesh or natural talents and abilities aren't even a part of the equation, and that's not an easy pill for many to swallow. That concept wasn't easy for me to digest either, but over time, I discovered that asking the "who" question brought me to a place of refuge and rest.

It was around 1999 when I entered a season of discontentment. I was getting up, going to work, collecting a paycheck and paying bills. And then... I was getting up, going to work, collecting a paycheck and paying bills. I was in my early 30s, and I started to realize I had another 34 or 35 years of this merry-go-round existence. I began to wonder:

God, is this all there is? Surely there's more to life than this. Surely I'm meant for more than this. God, why am I here? **What** *is my purpose?*

I didn't see it then, but I clearly see it now. For me to know my purpose and to live it out, I first needed to know *who* I was and, more specifically, *who* God said I was. The next thing I had to do was believe Him. This principle is true for every believer. When we know and truly believe we are who God says that we are, the attacks from Satan and other people bear no weight because they can't move us out of the position and title God has called us to.

In asking God what my purpose was and why I was here, I didn't get the immediate response I had hoped for. What I did get was a mathematical equation from a pastor's sermon:

"God's mathematics looks like this: $A + B + C = D$. God only gives you the 'A.' "

What?! That was definitely not what I wanted to hear!

As time went on, things didn't get any clearer. They actually became even more convoluted and confusing. I wanted the answers to my questions, and I wanted them *my* way—as in I wanted them fast and in a hurry. But God's ways and timing are not mine—and for that, I'm grateful.

OK, it's confession time here. What you've just read is hard-earned wisdom from a forty-something young woman. What you're about to read is a perfect storm of circumstances and events from a thirty-something young woman who had no clue about who she was and who allowed people and situations to define her. But, thank God that He had other plans for my life. The following is not what I would have prescribed...but hey, I'm not God.

To save us time, I'm just going to give you a running list of what I call the perfect storm that came crashing down on me over the course of a few years.

- After 34 years of marriage, my parents divorced. I was devastated.

- I began to make poor financial decisions, ultimately leading to bankruptcy.

- I became disenchanted with one job, and without consulting God, I left it for something else. In a year's time, I was jobless.

- My brother lost his job around the same time, and though we both struggled to hold on to our homes, he eventually lost his home and moved in with me.

- My home was nearly foreclosed on two or three times.

- I had friends walk away from me.

- I lost my awareness of and love for nature. Hearing birds sing became aggravating noise, not beautiful music. I just wanted them to *shut up*.

With all that I have just shared, can you imagine how I was feeling? I was scared. I was sad. I was hurt. I was depressed. I was alone. I was embarrassed. I was angry. My soul was empty, and I was just lost. It was a terrible time for me. I was in a cycle of despair. And though these labels didn't fit who

God said I was, I took them on as my identity nonetheless, and I didn't know how to remove myself from their yoke. Not until a divine encounter with, of all things, a butterfly.

Beautiful Butterfly

After losing my job and sleeping away the springtime, I grew tired of being cooped up in the house and decided to go for a walk with my dog, Rusty. The sun felt good warming my skin, and the fresh air rejuvenated me. About a block and a half into our walk, we approached the subdivision's model home. The yard was beautifully landscaped and the flowers were in their full glory. A protective netting rested over the flowers to keep deer from eating them. As I admired the flowers in the bed nearest me, something caught my eye. A butterfly was trapped under the netting, looking for a way out. The butterfly flew up as far as it could and then dropped back down. Up and back down, up and back down. I lifted the netting to free it, but, interestingly, it didn't fly away. It just kept going up and back down as though it was still trapped. This continued until the butterfly eventually stopped in the street not too far off the curb, but far enough out to potentially be run over. I started to pick it up to get it out of harm's way, but I had an overwhelming sense that I was to leave it there. Although I struggled with the decision, I couldn't deny the overpowering veto in my mind. So I left it there.

Rusty and I continued on our walk, but all the while, I wanted to go back to rescue that butterfly. Just the thought of it getting run over hit me in the pit of my stomach. As we headed back we walked by the same model home and I was afraid I would find the butterfly squashed in the road. I had such a sick feeling in my stomach. When we returned to the place I had left the butterfly, it was nowhere to be found. It had, I surmised, finally realized it was free and went back to doing what it was created to do.

Relieved, I asked God what that whole experience was about. This time, unlike when I had asked about my purpose, He immediately spoke to my heart: *So many of My people remain in bondage when, in fact, I have already set them free. They don't realize they're free and therefore don't live in the fullness of life that I've provided for them. They continue to live in the old pattern of up and down, up and down. But like that butterfly, they need to realize they are free, gather up their strength, and get back to being who I called them to be and doing what I called them to do.*

Life's situations and circumstances can easily lock us into a pattern that takes us up and down or round and round with no forward progress toward discovering who we really are as children of God. We can remain conditioned by the world's system, or we can be renewed by God's love and His plan. I've been renewed by God's love and have found the rest and refuge that my soul has longed for. You can find His love and mercy too. It all starts with knowing in your heart and declaring "I Am Who God Says I Am." And one thing I know for certain that God says about you—you are loved.

> *"For I am persuaded, that neither death, nor life, nor angels, nor principalities, nor powers, nor things present, nor things to come, Nor height, nor depth, nor any other creature, shall be able to separate us from the love of God, which is in Christ Jesus our Lord"* (Romans 8:38–39, KJV).

Beauty For Ashes Press

MOVING MOUNTAINS IN MARRIAGE

Beauty For Ashes Press

AFTER THE WEDDING
By Beverly Dru Lewis

It seems unreasonable to anticipate an event for years, and to plan and prepare for months—only to find yourself in the middle of the experience with a distinct feeling you are in over your head. That's where I found myself 36 years ago, just after the wedding—my wedding.

I had seen enduring marriages modeled by my parents and grandparents. So, I assumed I could slide easily into marriage, and I thought everything would work out fine. Instead, I discovered it is harder than it looks and more difficult than one imagines to be married—much less to live happily ever after.

Walt Disney didn't invent fairy tales; he just expanded their reach and put them in living color in almost every home in America. The expectation of an adoring prince charming coming to rescue a princess is ingrained in the psyche of every little girl through the timeless tool of storytelling. We grow up with dreams of gossamer gowns, glass slippers and a palace. Nothing in those familiar scenes prepare us for what's real. By the time I was a teenager, I was oblivious to my own unrealistic expectation of marriage, including the idea that someone perfect was going to come along and make my dreams come true.

Like thousands of newlyweds before me, I found myself living in a new town, job-seeking and adjusting to a totally unfamiliar life. Then, throw in the inevitable conflicts between two completely opposite personalities and the neediness created from loneliness, and it was really tough. Looking back, I realize I was selfish and demanding, though I certainly didn't recognize these traits back then. I just wanted to be happy. And, I wanted my husband to actively participate in making that happen. But here's a news flash: even a terrific husband makes a lousy God.

Fortunately, when I was hunting for happiness, I found God. It happened through a group of Christian women who befriended me. As I realized my need for a counselor, teacher, friend and Savior, I invited Christ into my heart. Though I didn't confess my struggle with learning to be a wife to my new friends, I was asked to facilitate a new Bible Study on building a Christ-centered home. I laughingly responded that I would attend but couldn't possibly lead it. God knew exactly what I needed, so in spite of my resistance, the group began with me leading. It seemed like a joke! I was so uncomfortable with the concepts in the material, that I most certainly would have quit attending had I not made a commitment to the group. I was uncharacteristically quiet during the sessions as I learned first-hand about the conviction the Holy Spirit brings to the heart.

God began to reveal that my need to be right (and oh, how I love to be right) is a spirit of pride. And, I had an unhealthy dose of it. He gently showed me that the only way I would see change in our marriage was to change the only person I was accountable for—myself.

It was fascinating to learn to discern the voice of God—He has so much to say! It's just that He usually whispers while the world roars. One of my early lessons from Him was about the power of words. A little song, based on Scripture (songs are always my fastest route to memorizing Bible verses) became a favorite. "Don't be moved by what you see, don't be moved by what you feel, but call those things that be not as though they were," based on Romans 4:17, ran through my mind day and night. It was a very real reminder to think about God and speak good things. After all, God spoke the universe into existence and then delegated to us the power to speak our world into order through our words.

God began to show me how to speak words of life to my husband, instead of what I had been doing: criticizing and pointing out where he was falling short. I learned that the tongue is a small part of the body, but it can be like fire. It's just like a small spark can burn up a whole forest (see James 3:5–8). I've started more than my share of fires with my tongue. If my tongue got shorter every time I've had to bite it, my tongue would almost be gone. I've learned the hard way not to say something permanently painful just because I'm temporarily angry.

Blaming Satan for our troubled homes can become a habit that distracts us from a more dangerous issue: self-absorption. The reality is that Satan can only hook us through our self-centeredness. Only dependence on God's life in us can protect us from self and thus shut the door to the enemy. I tell myself all the time, "Get over yourself—it's not about you." I want my life to be about Jesus and building the Kingdom of God on earth. I want to leave a legacy of love for our children and our children's children.

As time passed, the fact that Jim wasn't a Christian became a real sore spot. Unfortunately, I developed a religious attitude about this reality. It was yet another manifestation of pride. Since I was praying, reading my Bible, going to church and seeking wise counsel, I must be right and my husband must be wrong, correct? Nope – not even close. That's not the way it works. God wants us to honor our husbands.

Unfortunately, I loathed the word *submission*. That mentality doesn't sound spiritual, but it was the truth. My half-hippie liberal minded 25-year-old self just didn't get it. The truth is, most of Christiandom doesn't get it. We've got the world on one end of the spectrum shouting that a woman is self-sufficient and has all authority over her life and her body. Then there's the religious side espousing a doctrine that depicts woman as a weak doormat. I found the truth in the Bible. The husband and wife are to submit first to God, then to one another, according to Ephesians 5:21. Eve was taken out of the side of Adam to protect him from his aloneness. God designed woman to stand face-to-face with man and call him forth in a way no one else can. The intimacy of marriage is supposed to be the incubator for the fulfillment of our destiny. No wonder it can be so hard!

Ask God to tell you how He sees you and to describe what your role is—He will never demean or belittle you. You are amazing and wonderful! I learned to turn to God to get my deepest needs met. As a result, my husband was set free to love me the way only *he* can!

I'll never forget one day when I had a lesson on marriage while standing in church in the midst of praise and worship. Only I wasn't worshipping. I was murmuring and complaining. I was mad. Jim and I had an argument when I was trying to get out the door with the children, since he didn't go to church. I was sort of fussing at God, explaining to Him the unfairness of it all and telling God I just couldn't carry on with this "love your husband" bit any longer. That's when God interrupted me with a staggering message. He said, "I'm not asking you to love him." "Huh? What? Did I hear that right, God?" He replied, "I am asking you to let me love him through you." The revelation exploded in my understanding: I am just the hose. God is the water. I left that service refreshed. What a wonderful freedom to relax in the love of God and let Him do the work! That revelation was the gateway to loving others unconditionally. That image transformed our home and it changed my understanding of how to love others as well.

After 17 years of marriage, buckets of tears and countless prayers, my husband had a power encounter with the Living God. It's a little embarrassing to admit that I had given up on the hope of that event ever happening. Therein was a lesson: God is at work and responding to our prayers, even when we can't see anything happening. And God's timing is rarely in synch with our expectations. God set Jim's heart on fire and it has never dimmed or flickered. Interestingly, a wise pastor cautioned me when Jim was born again that happily ever-after had not arrived. He said that we needed to be aware that the Enemy of our souls would fight with every weapon available against the unstoppable power of a husband and wife who pray together in unity. It was indeed a tough year. But with God in our midst, the outcome was sure.

A marvelous thing happens over time when you learn to handle the heart of another with love and respect. You learn to forgive an offense when no apology is offered. You learn to overlook disappointment when you don't get your way and still keep a good attitude. You learn to "fight fair" by not accusing and blaming. You learn to gently articulate your needs without snapping. And you don't bring up a list of grievances when you are upset. You address one thing at a time. Have I mastered all this? Heavens, no! But I get the opportunity to start fresh every morning and walk it out. And it does become easier with time.

I've been able to remain teachable through the really tough lessons because of the goodness and grace of God. He loves us deeply and completely, even when we fall woefully short of His best. The term "ragamuffin gospel" is very real to me as I look at how he wooed this ragamuffin masquerading as a self-confident woman and tamed my rebellious heart. What is rebellion other than thinking that you know best? Rebelling is also trying to craft your own life by doing your own thing when the Master Builder has an impeccable plan. His blueprint will withstand the storms of life. Going your own way is sheer foolishness. Time is of the essence—and I don't want to waste it on foolishness.

There's a Kingdom to be built. He is with us every step of the way to give us joy and strength in the process. We get to be eyewitnesses of His glory as he patiently transforms flawed people into spotless brides. We get a glimpse of His majesty as we surrender our will and participate in the beauty that He has planned within the covenant of marriage.

God's promises are true! We can look forward to a mansion prepared for us in a city paved with streets of gold where we will live with the Prince of Peace and the King of Kings. That's a happily ever-after no fairy tale can touch.

I AM A SINNER OF THE WORST KIND
Anonymous

I am sinner of the worst kind. How is it that God could still love me after what I've done? I look back at all the bad decisions I've made (and believe me…there are many) and a few stand out as darker—uglier if you will—than others. This article highlights one of those uglier stories.

I was married to my husband in 1993 at 18 years old after fewer than 6 months of dating. Nothing other than the impulsivity of youth brought us to wed so young and so quickly. We had a great relationship in every way. My husband is and always has been a wonderful man: he is so incredibly handsome, honest, kind, strong and a great life partner. Few women could want for more.

However, after 12 years of marriage, I was far from walking hand-in-hand with my husband, and I was far from walking hand-in-hand with my Lord. I was much more interested in drinking, doing drugs, partying and flirting. I wasn't just flirting with men, but I was flirting with disaster. It was such a rush to find the attention of a new man. I did not want to be married. I did not want to be tied down. I wanted to have fun. I wanted to fulfill my lustful desire to "live in the flesh." I sought out and found the sexual affair that I wanted. Satan was so willing to accommodate the desires that pulled me away from my loving Heavenly Father. And I was so willing to jump right into bed with another man.

The relationship that I was so excitedly involved in continued for 11 months. It was chock full of the highs of sneaking around and pushing boundaries to see what I could get away with. It was also chalked full of lies about my whereabouts, excuses for extra time spent at work and me selfishly inflicting pain on so many people who I loved. I thought I was happy...living so carnally...and having so much fun!

After a long chain of ugly events (which included a STD scare), the affair ended. Something changed in me. It changed almost overnight. It changed without explanation, and quite suddenly. I knew that I had to tell my husband about what I'd done. I knew what was at stake, but there was a pull in me to "do the right thing" and be honest. My husband's response was one of pain, disappointment—and not surprisingly—anger. We agreed that a separation was in order.

During our six-month separation, I began to pray. I prayed to a God on whom I'd long since turned my back. I was called to memorize several scriptures:

"Marriage should be honored by all, and the marriage bed be kept pure, for God will judge the adulterer and all the sexually immoral" (Hebrews 13:4, NIV)

"For the wages of sin is death, but the free gift of God is eternal life in Christ Jesus our Lord" (Romans 6:23, NIV).

"If we confess our sins, he is faithful and just and will forgive us our sins and purify us from all unrighteousness" (1 John 1:9, NIV).

I was called to a deeper closeness with friends who would point me towards Christ. Not only did I seek forgiveness and reconciliation from my husband, but I sought it from my loving Father above. God gave me a husband with a huge heart, and He led my husband to forgive me. God, of course, forgave me from the moment I breathed my humiliated, contrite prayer. He was doing a work in me...a work to draw me closer to Him.

For quite some time, I found it extremely hard to forgive myself. Jesus died on the cross to pay for MY sins. He took the lashings, the pain, the humiliation, the crucifixion and death for MY lustful desires and behavior. It was so hard to carry the guilt of knowing how I'd hurt Him and how I'd turned my back on Him. The Holy Spirit spoke to me, saying that if Christ endured all of that so my sins would be forgiven (should I ask), who am I to not honor and acknowledge that? He wanted to forgive me, and He wanted me to forgive myself. What kind of God does that? Certainly not the God I learned about as a little girl: a cold, stark, condemning God! I grew up believing that there were degrees of sin...that one sin was worse than another. The sin of infidelity was the worst of the worst and the ultimate betrayal of marriage and God. "Once a cheater, always a cheater," in the eyes of the god of my youth. Slowly I started to see that our Savior does not operate in this manner. *"If my people, who are called by my name, will humble themselves and pray and seek my face and turn from their wicked ways, then I will hear from heaven and I will forgive their sin and heal their land"* (2 Chronicles 7:14, NIV). This God was a huge, glorious God who not only forgave me, but He also led my husband to forgive me, and showed me that it was right in His eyes to forgive myself. What a gracious and mighty God! I am in awe of how miraculously He protected me through such a vile season in my life. As far away as I strayed, He sought to complete a work in me that would draw me closer to Him.

Fast forward to 2015. My husband and I are closer than ever, and are about to celebrate 22 years of marriage. I'm still amazed at how God can take such an awful situation and use it for His good, and my own good. Without facing the threat of losing my husband, I don't know that I would have ever been humbled enough to seek God and discover who He really is and what He's done for us. My husband and I are one, and Christ dwells in the center of our relationship now. It is because of the work that He's done in me and in us that we are happy and seek Him in our daily lives. He taught me that forgiveness is possible. He saved me. He saved my marriage. He saved us as a couple: a couple whom He joined together for life.

I am sinner of the worst kind. Yet, God loves me even after all that I've done because He is perfect and unfailing in forgiveness, grace and mercy. He loves me despite all of the ugliness in me.

PERSEVERING WITH UNIMAGINABLE PEACE

Beauty For Ashes Press

CANCER
By Vanessa Hlavaty

Approximately 60 days after the adoption of our first and only child, I found a lump under my left arm. I knew this was no cyst, no ingrown hair, no run of the mill lump. I knew this was something serious. Within three days, and at the age of 37, I was in my doctor's office, where I was scheduled for my first mammogram.

After a lumpectomy, a lymph node biopsy, and a visit to Texas for a second opinion, I was diagnosed with stage three advanced breast cancer. I could give you the gory medical details of my diagnosis (the specific type of cancer, chemotherapy, radiation, a double mastectomy, etc...) and the grim prognosis for remission, but that's not the point of this story. The point of this story is to tell you, the reader, how clearly I see God and his plan for my life, and how thankful I am for his sovereignty.

After a life full of painfully broken relationships, addiction, bankruptcy, infidelity, infertility and failed adoptions, I see His beautiful plan unfolding on a daily basis. After the initial shock of a life threatening diagnosis wore off, I was left feeling hopeful. Peaceful. Comforted. I know this response is not normal, but I felt the Holy Spirit telling me that He's shown me time and time again that His plan is perfect. His plan is so much better than my plan. His plan may be to call me home a whole lot earlier than I ever expected. His plan may be to keep me on this planet to share with people what I know to be true about our all powerful, merciful, forgiving God. Whatever it is, I'm brought to hopeful, happy tears as I type this. I'm hopeful and happy knowing that He's in control. Oh what a relief to be loved by a merciful and sovereign God.

"Therefore I tell you, do not worry about your life, what you will eat or drink; or about your body, what you will wear. Is not life more than food, and the body more than clothes? Look at the birds of the air; they do not sow or reap or store away in barns, and yet your heavenly Father feeds them. Are you not much more valuable than they? Can any one of you by worrying add a single hour to your life?" (Matthew 6:25–27, NIV).

CHRISTOPHER
By Susan Sexton

It was a cold, dreary December day and I was at home spending the morning with my family. There was nothing all that special about that particular Friday with the exception of my husband being home. Since it was so close to the end of the year, he had vacation time that he needed to use. Today was one of those days. He could stay with our active two-year-old son, while I ran errands and went to my 35-week pregnancy check-up. I had been anxious about this appointment. Two days earlier, I considered being seen because my baby's movements had changed. Everything I read, however, reassured me that I was being overly worried. After all, you couldn't compare pregnancies and babies move differently as they grow bigger and descend further into your pelvis. I just needed the official confirmation that all was well. Christmas was just three days away and I wanted so badly to enjoy the season and shake that ominous feeling. My new addition was set to arrive on January 22, and I couldn't wait for my boys to finally meet each other.

As my son played nearby that morning, my husband was in and out doing things around the house. I was working on my computer and an episode of *All in the Family* was playing in the background. I really didn't care for that show too much. It was more than 30 years old, and I just couldn't identify with the characters. However, I was too busy to find the remote to change the channel so on it played. I overheard Archie's daughter, Gloria, announce that she was pregnant. Archie was furious because Gloria and her husband had been living with him since they had no way to support themselves. He thought the pregnancy was very irresponsible. By the end of the episode, I had become increasingly attentive and Archie actually started to warm up to the idea of being a grandfather. Sadly, Gloria miscarried her baby and there was a very moving scene between father and daughter. I remember thinking how grateful I was to have never suffered a miscarriage. I left for my appointment at the end of the episode. As I drove, I felt the reassuring movements of my baby, which seemed to ease my mind.

The OB/GYN practice I went to was large, and that day, I would be seeing a doctor I had never seen before. The doctors preferred to see you on a rotational basis throughout your pregnancy because there was no guarantee which doctor would be on-call when you delivered. I had heard good things about Dr. M. In fact, my husband attended middle school for a brief time with her and had graduated from high school with her sister. They were from a small town where everyone knows or knows of each other. As I sat in the exam room waiting to be seen, I could hear the steady beat of the fetal heart rate monitor next door. Another mother like me was checking in on the child she carried.

It felt like forever before the knock came at my exam room door signaling that the doctor was ready to see me. Dr. M walked in and introduced herself. I instantly liked her because she was very down-to-earth and friendly. After the usual small talk, I shared with her that I had begun to worry about my son because his movements had changed. She reassured me that this was not uncommon later in pregnancy. I was excited as she laid the fetal heart rate monitor across my abdomen. As Dr. M began searching for his heartbeat, I became unnerved as the seconds ticked by without success. I saw it in her face too. After what felt like forever, she calmly suggested we try the portable ultrasound machine she had down the hall. As I waited for her to come back in, I told myself this was crazy. After all, I had just felt him move on my way to the appointment. I was in complete denial and would not allow myself to consider the fears I had felt that week. I never really believed them, did I? How could anything go wrong in a perfectly normal, textbook pregnancy? Dr. M returned quickly with the ultrasound machine and went right to work. Still, there was no heartbeat. It was as if she too was refusing to believe it could be possible. Dr. M calmly told me not to panic but that we should go straight to the ultrasound wing of the practice where they had much more sophisticated machines than her portable one. As I bent down to put my shoes back on, I felt him move! It was a precious glimmer of hope. Since Dr. M was still in the room, I had her come and feel my abdomen. To this day, I remember the look on her face as she informed me that it wasn't him moving as I believed all along—it was simply a contraction. At that moment, it all began to sink in. These changing "movements" I had felt all week were nothing more than contractions. Down the hall we rushed, and I was whisked into a more advanced ultrasound room. The technician turned on her machine and made no eye contact with me. It only took a few seconds to confirm what was becoming all too clear now. There was no sign of life. Her eyes met Dr. M's and she shook her head no. Dr. M's hands went up as she cupped her face in horror. All she could do was repeat over and over "I'm so sorry. I'm so sorry."

I didn't know how to react because shock had completely taken over. "What am I supposed to do now?" is what I heard come out of my mouth. Dr. M told me that I could either go on to the hospital to be induced or I could go home over the weekend and come back Monday for induction. *Go home?* There was no way I could go home knowing he was gone. I wanted him out so we could find out what had gone wrong. I asked if the ultrasound technician could see any visible issues. I really needed answers. She told me that due to my advanced stage of pregnancy, the baby was too large for her to see everything in my womb. Dr. M asked her to at least check on the umbilical cord. From what the technician could see, it looked ok.

My mind was reeling. What had I done wrong? Had I not prayed enough for this child? Did I ignore the signs that he was in distress and miss the chance to have saved him? This was my second pregnancy: How on earth could I not have known the difference between a movement and a contraction? I was his mother and it was my responsibility to take care of him, yet I had failed him. In the midst of my swirling thoughts, Dr. M shared with me that this same thing had happened to her sister a few years before at 38 weeks. The same thing had happened to the very same sister my husband knew. As it turned out, Dr. M was scheduled to work at the hospital that evening so she would be there to induce me. She knew on a personal level what a profound loss it was since she watched her sister suffer through a stillbirth. God could not possibly have placed a better doctor into my life for that moment.

The time had finally come for me to call my husband. I imagined him at home blissfully unaware that our lives were about to change. Dr. M volunteered to make that phone call, but I knew I had to do it. I was escorted into a private office, where trembling, I dialed home. As soon as my husband answered, it was as if all the emotion I had been holding back burst forth into a flood of tears. I guess saying it out loud finally made it real. "I've lost the baby" was about all I could say through sobs. He was completely stunned and told me he would be right there as soon as he dropped our son off with his parents. I wanted to meet him in the parking lot because I desperately needed to get out of that office and just be alone. The hospital was connected to my doctor's office, but I couldn't bear to walk into the labor and delivery unit alone—I just couldn't.

When I made it out to the privacy of my car, I was in such despair. I took out my cell phone and called my parents. My father answered, but I needed to talk to my mother. I tried to sound as if nothing were wrong and calmly asked to speak to mom. As I heard her voice, my emotions took over as I explained the events that had transpired. I told her that my husband was on his way, and that it needed to be just the two of us that night at the hospital. My grief alone was overwhelming, and I couldn't stand to see the sadness etched on my parents' faces as we awaited the stillbirth of our son.

When my husband finally arrived, we cried together and tried to make sense of what had happened. We attempted to regain our composure for the walk into the hospital. When we arrived at Labor and Delivery to check-in, there lay a newborn in a nursery cart being tended to by a nurse. Our hearts sank. It was a stark reminder of what we had lost. I would soon be delivering a child we could not take home. While parents all around us were celebrating the happiest moment of their lives, we were mourning the worst day of ours.

The hospital staff ushered us quickly into a delivery suite. They were so attentive and deeply sympathetic. I was given an IV and was hooked up to different monitors. The hardest thing was looking at the straight line on the screen where there should've been my baby's heartbeat. I willed it to move and prayed fervently that a miracle would happen. Maybe it was all just a terrible mistake. It didn't take long for the labor-inducing drug to take effect, and my contractions began. I was given an epidural almost simultaneously because they didn't want me to feel any physical pain. It was evident that I was already in great emotional distress.

It was a long, miserable night. I laid awake the entire time even though I was given a sleeping pill. It was as if my grief would not allow me the escape that sleep provided. My husband and I sat up talking for a long time. He listened as I recounted every moment I could recall of the last week. A grief nurse was sent in to walk us through all the options we had. It was all just so overwhelming. We had to think about whether we wanted an autopsy to be conducted. My head was spinning with sadness and indecision. Dr. M informed us that they would be conducting all kinds of lab tests on me, the baby and the placenta even if we decided against the autopsy. There was no guarantee an autopsy would tell us anything unless there was a physical defect. We decided to hold off on making the final decision until his delivery and were hoping to have more answers by then. As the night progressed, there was a moment when my husband fell asleep and I was alone with my thoughts. A night nurse walked in to check on me and I collapsed into her arms in hysterical sobs. The weight of this reality was too much to endure. She was just what I needed that night—a shoulder to cry on. God had sent this wonderful staff to take care of me in my greatest time of need.

Dr. M was still working at the hospital the next morning when it was time for me to deliver. At 5:08 a.m. on December 23rd, I delivered our beloved Christopher, weighing 4 pounds, 11 ounces,. and measuring 19 inches long. Dr. M. discovered that his umbilical cord had wrapped around his neck twice very tightly and at such an angle that it was declared the cause of his death. As a result, we decided against an autopsy. He was so beautiful and my husband and I spent the morning holding him. We called our families, and invited them to come in and see him as well. It was a very emotional morning for everyone. Before Dr. M'.s shift ended, she came in to talk with us about everything. She had to be exhausted, but she patiently answered every question we had and offered to get me in touch with her sister so the healing process could begin. She told me that it was not normal policy to release a patient on the same day of her delivery, but she would make an exception for me if I wanted to go home. That was the best news of the day. I wanted nothing more than to retreat to the comfort of home, and I wanted to see our surviving son. It felt surreal being wheeled out of the hospital with no child in my arms.

The days that followed were a blur. I plastered a fake smile on my face for the sake of my 2-year-old son. I just wanted him to have a "Merry" Christmas. Behind closed bedroom doors, I would sob into my pillow. The additional cruelty of a stillbirth is that your body produces milk because it doesn't know your child was lost. Then there is the reality of all the clothes and baby things you have to put away—just more painful reminders.

We buried Christopher on December 27th with just our immediate families present. Inviting others was just too much for us at that time. Our pastor read various wonderful passages but the one I loved the most was John 14:1-4, NIV:

"Do not let your hearts be troubled. You believe in God; believe also in me. ² My Father's house has many rooms; if that were not so, would I have told you that I am going there to prepare a place for you? ³ And if I go and prepare a place for you, I will come back and take you to be with me that you also may be where I am. ⁴ You know the way to the place where I am going."

I have such peace knowing that my Savior prepared a place for Christopher as He does for all that call upon Him. That knowledge sustained me in the days and months that followed. It wasn't always easy though. There were days that I didn't want to get out of bed because I was so consumed by the "whys" and "what ifs." On those days, I would look to Scripture, pray or go through the wonderful cards we received from family and friends. One card in particular helped me so much. It was from a member of our church family. She wrote, "I hope you can feel the prayers all around you." The truth is that I could feel them. Even in my darkest hour, I felt peace. Sometimes that peace felt so out of place in the midst of my turmoil—yet it was there. In fact, I never felt his comforting presence more than I did at that sad time of my life.

The words of Psalm 34:18 were never so true as it was for me then:

"The Lord is close to the brokenhearted and saves those who are crushed in spirit" (Psalm 34:18, NIV).

That time of despair gave me a whole new appreciation for the son I still had. I cherished every milestone and enjoyed him even more than I thought possible. He was such a bright spot in that dark time and brought joy I thought was lost forever. As painful as this experience was, I can look back and see that God was holding my hand every step of the way. I truly believe that He puts people in our path to be His hands and feet. God placed so many to help me on my personal journey through grief. It started with my doctor and continued with a host of others. That's how He works. A time came later when, much to my dismay, I found myself strongly convicted to share my story of loss with a group of women at Bible study. It was agonizing, but as it turned out, one of the ladies had just suffered a stillbirth, and she badly needed to hear my story. Sometimes we find ourselves in a season as the one in need. There will also come a season when we must serve those in need. No matter the season of your life, God is always there. You just need to look for Him. Nearly 13 months after the loss of Christopher, we welcomed a precious baby girl. She is truly our beauty from the ashes. I will always miss the son that I lost, and I think often about what he would be like. I know that someday I'll hold him in Heaven, but for now, it's my Heavenly Father who holds me.

Beauty For Ashes Press

VENGEANCE IS MINE, SAITH THE LORD
By Linda Bingham

It was early in 1998 and Danny and I were beginning our life together. We were engaged to be married while living together, and we had just started attending a little Assembly of God church up the street from our home. We were merging two families: my son and daughter with his two daughters. We wanted to start our new life right in the eyes of God. So we spoke to the preacher of the church about marrying us, but we wanted to go through marriage counseling before we got married. This step was important to us since neither of us wanted another failed marriage. We began our journey to becoming one in the eyes of God, as well as rededicating our lives to the Lord. That combination set Satan on a rampage to keep us from moving forward in our new life together and from fulfilling God's will for our lives.

April 17, 1998, is a day that will forever be marked in my mind. It was a typical Friday, springtime afternoon. I had gone into town to have lunch with my fiancée, who is now my husband. Shortly after taking him back to work, I began my journey home. We lived a few miles out of town, and my phone rings. It was my best friend who jokingly says, "Hey girl, I don't know what you did, but why didn't you invite me so we both could have some fun?" Inquisitively, I asked "What are you talking about, and what rumors are you hearing now?" Then she seriously said: "My mom just called me. She heard on the scanner that the police department is looking for you. They are trying to serve a warrant on you."

My heart sank, my mind raced, anxiety was building, and of course I am reaching into the depths of my memory thinking: *Did I forget to pay a ticket? Did I do something when I was a teenager that is just now surfacing, What in the world could I have a warrant for my arrest?* Panic mode is in full swing as I quickly turn the car around and head back to Danny's work in full tears. I was shaking, trying to figure out why this was happening. As I walk into his work to explain, he immediately picks up the phone and calls his good friend, who is the Sheriff. He explains the situation to him. Danny was told to have me go straight home and wait by the phone while the Sheriff finds out what is going on. After a couple hours, I get the call from the Sheriff. My instructions were: "Please come straight to the Sheriff's office. There is a warrant for your arrest. Go the back way off major highways, and I will be waiting for you."

As I walk into the Sheriff's department, I still have no idea what is happening or why I am being arrested. Tears are now a constant flood streaming down my cheeks. As I look up, a great friend of mine, who was one of the police officers was standing there. He offered to take the warrant to the Sheriff's office—my friend was my angel in blue that day. He quickly wraps his arms around me and says, "It's all going to be OK, you are being arrested because your ex-husband has filed charges on you for phone harassment."

Puzzled, confused, scared and perplexed are just a few of the emotions that were hovering around me. It was my ex-husband's attempt to gain custody of our children by making me look like an unfit mother.

As we are talking, the Sheriff, another angel, comes to the door and takes me by the hand to go in the back for processing. He explains that this action is the procedure and they must do it. But, he has secured a judge to arraign me for immediate release. I was not going to have to stay in jail overnight, nor was I going to be in a holding cell. Numbness has now set in, and I felt as if I am watching a lifetime movie being played out—but it is my life, and it is real.

After what seemed like a mile of hallways, loud slamming steel doors, hollow echoing walls, we rounded the corner to the booking room, there across the cold sterile table sat another angel—the Judge. I had become friends with him through my work as a sales rep for a local radio station. Because he owned a local business, he was one of my advertising clients. He asked me to sit down and quickly took me by the hand and said, "You don't have to worry about anything, you won't be staying here, this is all standard procedure. We will have to do some paperwork, get your fingerprints and mug shots. You will not have to worry about paying any money because I am placing you on a PR bond and you will be released immediately." I remember the judge never let go of my hand the whole time he was doing paperwork. He was so sweet to me. He was a small comfort to me in the middle Satan's attempt to gain a foot hold where he clearly knew he was loosing it.

Monday morning came and I was to report to the courthouse, where I was told that they have all the proof they need to convict me. I could go the jail, but the best thing for me to do was to plead guilty. This plea would place me on deferred adjudication. After stewing over this decision for an entire weekend, the anger had risen up within me. I quickly stood up, slammed my hands on his desk and looked the gentlemen square in the eyes across his desk and said, "I am not guilty, I never harassed anyone and I will not plead guilty to something I didn't do."

I was raised knowing right is right and wrong is wrong, with a God fearing mother who always told us that the truth shall set you free. Pleading guilty to a crime that I didn't commit wasn't going to happen, and being railroaded out of fear by Satan was never going to happen. I serve a bigger God that that! Even when I had turned my back on him for a few years of my life, God knew His child was coming home and He wouldn't leave me.

So with my plea of not guilty, a juror trial would likely be the next step. I requested a pro-bono attorney. As I waited in the hallway, I prayed for a specific attorney, who I knew was the best in town. The clerk handed me a card and said, "This will be your attorney. He is in the courthouse now, so you can talk to him, if you would like." The appointed attorney wasn't the one I prayed for, but I met with him. As we were talking, he asked my ex-husbands name and quickly said, "I can't take this case because he spoke to me about representing him during your divorce, and that would be a conflict of interest."

So, I was back to square one sitting in the hall waiting for another appointed attorney. I was still praying for the one who I knew was the best. At that moment—God never fails—the next card that was handed to me was the attorney who I had prayed about. What happened in the case? Well, let's just say: God is good - ALL the time.

I will take a minute to explain the phone harassment, though. I had called my ex-husband's house on two occasions and his new wife hung up on me. Once was when our daughter was home sick from school. He was supposed to pick her up after school, but clearly, he couldn't because she wasn't there. The second time I called was during the month our children had visitation with their dad. I wanted to hear their voices so I called to talk to them. I was also hung up on then. It is a good thing that I had documentation of the two dates I was arrested for, since these calls were made from my phone. A phone tap was placed on their line for 18 months. During that time, my ex-husband and his wife were going around town on pay phones, calling their house and hanging up when the answering machine picked up. These calls resulted in hundreds of phone calls. They, then tried to claim that I was the one calling.

During the next few months, Danny and I got married. We still attended our little Assembly of God Church, where no one knew what was happening, and I tried my best to carry on with some normalcy for my children, who also didn't know that these events had happened. I never wanted them to feel unsafe. As the days drew closer to the trial date, I prayed and prayed for God to let me know that I was going to be with my children and not in jail.

A month before we were to go to trial, I was driving through town on a Monday morning. A church sign read, "Vengeance is mine saith the Lord." (That statement can be found in the King James Version of Romans 12:19.) That Wednesday night, we went to church as usual. We sat down behind the sweetest elderly couple and after church she turned around and said to me, "I have no idea why, but God has told me all night to tell you, 'Vengeance is mine saith the Lord.' " Immediate tears start to flow as I knew God was in the details. Over the course of the few days, God spoke to my heart to call the preacher's wife, share what was happening and ask her to pray for the situation. As I began to share the story with her she interrupted me and said, "*Vengeance is mine saith the Lord.*" I knew then I was going to be fine because God is in the details.

Nine months and finally the trial date had arrived. The jurors were selected and testimonies began. Numb and still watching this Lifetime movie play out in my real life I sat in the courtroom waiting to hear the fate of my life. My ex-husband and his wife couldn't be in the courtroom when the other was testifying. Their stories were not the same. A couple of police officers testified. They were asked if they knew my ex-husband was behind on child support for two years, would that have made a difference in this case. There was a resounding yes. When I was questioned about the two dates on their 18-month phone tap, I could show documentation of why I called them. After a couple hours of testimonies the jurors were released to determine guilt or innocence. The verdict was brought back quickly, and I was found not guilty of phone harassment.

God is in the details, I wasn't arrested, handcuffed and escorted to jail in the back of a police car. I wasn't locked up in jail until Monday morning. I was only waiting for a judge to return to work after the weekend. I was given a bond that I never had to pay back and a lawyer pro-bono. I was given the opportunity to grow in my faith and stand on God's Word, knowing I never had to harbor anger, vengeance, shame or bitterness towards my ex-husband and his wife, because "vengeance is mine, saith the Lord."

I know walking through the trials of life can be a heavy burden to bare. No matter if you are fighting to prove your innocence after being falsely accused of a crime or just trying to live each day battling Satan as he tries to take control of your life. Nothing can compare to walking in the light and knowing no matter what fate awaits, in the outcome of your life, God is always in the details. Look to find them.

YOU GOT YOUR GIRL
By Jennifer Waddle

The critical care nurses gave her the name, "Baby Goliath." Even though she was only five pounds, she looked huge compared to the other sick babies in the unit.

Hours earlier, my husband had witnessed the birth of our only daughter, and had leaned over to whisper, "You got your girl."

With two boys at home, we were overjoyed that God had blessed us with little Hannah. Yes, she was a few weeks early, but doctors had determined that her lungs were developed and she was ready to be born. It was good for me, as I had been battling preterm labor for days.

Hannah was born with a full head of dark hair, rosy cheeks and a *scowl*. Her furrowed brow would become her signature expression in the days to come. She was placed in my arms and I kissed her, thanking God again and again.

The nurse, busy with other things, happened to peer over my shoulder and immediately said, "Here, I need to take her for a minute." And before we knew it, more nurses were coming in, as well as doctors and other staff members.

Hannah was gasping for air. It seemed that something was blocking her airway. They suctioned and suctioned, finally rushing her to the NICU to be intubated. Of course, we were worried to death. My husband followed the nurses, trying to stay as close to our baby as possible.

When I was able, I went to the NICU to get an update. Seeing my newborn hooked up to all the tubes was horrible. I felt like I was in a dream—a very bad dream.

The doctor on call came over and ushered us to another room. He said there was a *mass* coming down behind the soft pallet and blocking her airway. He then said something that shocked us to the core. He said that it was possible that the bones at the bottom of her skull had not fused together and her brain was actually coming down, literally, into her throat.

We were sick. We clung to each other, not having a clue what the next days would hold.

The doctor left quickly, stating they would do a CT scan to determine what the mass really was.

The next several hours blurred one into the other. I was on my feet practically from the moment I delivered her. Weary and helpless, the news finally came.

The mass was a benign tumor called a Teratoma. Her brain was fine, but she would need to have surgery. They immediately sent her to the children's hospital. We drove home to quickly pack a bag and say goodbye to our boys. At ages five and six, they didn't understand what was happening to their tiny sister. I felt so torn leaving them behind. My emotions were all over the place, and I was physically exhausted.

By the time we got to the hospital, the sweet nurses had bathed her and put a tiny white bow in her hair. I cried when I saw it. That simple gesture meant so much!

The next day, we met the doctor who would be performing Hannah's surgery. She informed us that she had dealt with this kind of tumor before, but she warned us that it was in a very difficult place. She went on to say that it was possible Hannah would never speak or swallow. The tumor was pressing against one of her ear tubes and there was a risk of deafness in that ear. There was also the possibility that the nerves in her face would be damaged. Those were the risks of such an invasive surgery on such a little baby.

The day of the surgery, we were surrounded by family and friends. The medical staff prayed over our daughter, which both surprised and comforted us. The surgery took longer than expected, and when I finally saw her, I had to cry. She was so very pale and swollen. Her little tongue was hanging out because of the swelling. It was awful.

It was then that my faith in God was tested beyond anything I'd ever gone through. I sensed Him telling me that I would need to trust Him fully, even if He chose to take her to Heaven. It was as if He was asking me, "Will you still say that I am good if I take your daughter from you?"

That thought frightened me. It overwhelmed me. It made me want to beg and plead and cry. It challenged my beliefs and tested my faith.

But God...

God in His great love and perfect plan, brought me to a place where I was able to surrender my baby completely to Him. I remember leaning over the plastic, hospital bassinet, and with a broken heart and hoarse voice, singing, "God is so good... God is so good...God is so good, He's so good to me."

Over and over I sang that chorus. And each time, I believed it a little bit more than the time before.

Hannah did recover. During the next few days, we discovered that she was able to swallow, make sounds and hear. The nerves in her face were not damaged. Two weeks later she came home. She came home to meet her older brothers and settle in as part of our family.

Our "Baby Goliath" had defeated her own giant.

She is now ready to turn 16. She will be driving soon. She is beautiful and precious, and she reminds us every day that our God is merciful and mighty.

And every once in a while, when I stop to remember those difficult days, I see how the Lord brought us through, and I remember His peace in the midst of all the fear and desperation.

It was as if He leaned down and said, "You got your girl."

PRAYING POWERFUL PRAYERS

Beauty For Ashes Press

GOD'S PLAN FOR OUR FAMILY
By Vanessa Hlavaty

"I prayed for this child, and the Lord has granted me what I asked of Him" (1 Samuel 1:27, NIV)

From the time we married at the age of 18, my husband and I wanted a family. We envisioned ourselves with three or four children and eventually more grandchildren than we could count. For years we tried to conceive, to no avail. Ultimately we found ourselves part of the "secret society" of folks who are labeled infertile. All of the things that come to mind when one receives this diagnosis went through my mind: *Why me? Why us? What's wrong with me? What's wrong with him? What the heck are we going to do? Why do those losers-parents over there get to have kids, and we can't? Why would you do this to us, God?*

Initially, we tried fertility treatments, but decided it simply wasn't for us. Something stirred in my heart telling me there was a different path. That path was the long— sometimes heartbreaking—process of adoption.

Our first attempt to adopt was after a mission trip to an orphanage in Mexico. We met and fell in love with a sibling group of three children: two girls and one boy. After two trips to the orphanage, we developed a relationship with these children and our hearts were set on making them a part of our family. Once we returned from our second trip to Mexico, we immediately contacted a home study and adoption agency that a friend recommended. Although we knew it could take quite some time, we were ready to dig in our heels and bring our kiddos home. After several months of waiting on the Mexican government to consider our case, we were told that adoptions to US citizens were unofficially suspended from adopting Mexican children…suspended indefinitely. Our hearts broke. We cried. And then we cried some more. *How could this happen?* It was another blow from God that I didn't understand. Another chapter was closed.

Several months later we decided to pursue an international adoption from Ethiopia. We requested a little boy and moved forward knowing, again, that it would be a long process, but we were not dissuaded. We would have our family come hell or high water. In the summer of 2010, we contacted the home study and adoption agencies and started resubmitting all of our paperwork. Two days before Christmas that same year, we received another devastating blow: our home study AND adoption agencies were both going out of business. Not only had we lost the dream of our son, but we'd also lost our money!

To say that my heart was full of bitterness would be an understatement. Sometimes it's hard for me to find adequate words to describe just how low I felt. My bitterness at God's plan ran so deep. I wanted nothing to do with His plan…His stupid plan that left me and my husband childless. I refused to pray. I refused to turn to His word. I just couldn't bear it. As far as I was concerned, He'd clearly turned His back on us.

However, shortly after New Year's of 2011, I felt a small stirring in my heart. The kind of stirring that if maybe I could strike some sort of "deal" with God, He'd see fit to give us a child. (Misguided, I know.) But a few days later, a dear friend sent me an email. She typed one sentence that read, *"I prayed for this child, and the Lord has granted me what I asked of Him"* (1 Samuel 1:27, NIV). This verse hit me like a ton of bricks. A few days later a different friend sent me an email. In it, she reminded me of the following scripture,

"Religion that God our Father accepts as pure and faultless is this: to look after orphans and widows in their distress and to keep oneself from being polluted by the world" (James 1:27, NIV). I felt the Holy Spirit speaking to me that our journey was not over. My husband and I decided that we would sign up to become foster parents, and we would see what the Lord had in store for us.

We did 10 weeks of classes and started our home study. I wish I could say that I was confident in God's plan, but I wasn't. I knew that I wanted a child to take care of. I knew that I'd be devastated if a child were placed with us and then returned to his/her birth parents. And I knew that we had to try. In June 2011, we received "the call." A six-week old baby boy was at the hospital and he needed a foster family. He was born five weeks premature and was opiate dependent. His poor little body was exposed to heroin, methadone and other opiates in utero. He spent the first six weeks of his life detoxing in the NCIU, and he was in pretty bad shape.

We spent several months taking our son to visits with his birth mother. I'd sit quietly in the room listening to a social worker tell her what a good job she was doing on her path to recovery and that she'd have her son back in no time. I remember my heart felt like it was cracking in two under the pain that this child could be taken from us. I hit my knees night after night asking God to please give this child to us permanently. In that prayer time, two things were revealed to me:

1) This child would never be solely ours…no matter who he ended up with, he was God's child first and foremost. We were lucky to have him for as long as God saw fit.

2) I was overcome with guilt knowing that in my prayer for him to stay with us, I was ultimately praying for his birth mother to fail in her attempt at sobriety.

After 18 months of birth parent visits, countless court appearances, meetings with social workers and what felt like unending worry, a judge declared us our son's new, legal parents.

I think about the scriptures my friends sent to me, and I'm ashamed that I didn't believe in His plan for us all along. Even if His plan didn't include children, I wish I could go back and tell the me of 20 years ago to trust in His perfect overarching plan for my life. What if we'd had success with our fertility treatments? What it we'd adopted the children from Mexico? If there had been any shift in our path we wouldn't have our perfect son (and by perfect, please know that I mean he's perfect for US...not that he's a perfect child). My understanding of God's plan for His children radically changed. *"Sovereign Lord, you are God! Your covenant is trustworthy, and you have promised these good things to your servant"* (2 Samuel 7:28, NIV). I know beyond a shadow of a doubt that His timing and grace are far better than what I could ever choose for myself. If it weren't for this difficult journey, I don't know that I'd be able to understand Him as clearly as I do now. I'm so thankful for the pain and loss that we experienced so that I can be even more thankful for His continuing provision for me.

THE PRAYER OF JABEZ SHOULD COME WITH A WARNING LABEL
By Dr. Lori M. Hobson

The Prayer of Jabez is a very small passage in one of the less popular books of the bible. It says. "And Jabez called on the GOD of Israel saying, *'Oh that You would bless me indeed and enlarge my territory, that Your hand would be with me, and that You would keep me from evil, that I would not cause pain!'* So GOD granted him what he requested" (1 Chronicles 4:10, NKJV).

What an amazingly powerful little prayer! This story is a part of my personal testimony. Everyone who knows me well has heard this story. It is something that I share with everyone who will listen, usually beginning with the following statement. "I think the prayer of Jabez should have a warning label just like the ones on cigarettes and prescription medications." In my opinion, this story is the most important life reflection in my book, *Momma Sayings and Life Reflections*.

Several years ago, I was at the Dollar Store standing in the book aisle. A man whom I had never seen before, and never saw again, walked up to me and another woman and said, "You should buy this book. It is at the bookstore next door for $12.99, and we have it here for a dollar. It is a great book and you should buy it!"

I took the book down from the shelf and looked at it. It was *The Prayer of Jabez,* by Bruce Wilkinson. At first, I thought it was a children's book. As I thumbed through the beautifully illustrated pages, I realized that it was not a children's book, and it was about some kind of prayer. I thought, "Why not? It is only a dollar," and decided to buy it.

I took it home and tossed it, unopened, on my nightstand. I didn't think any more about it.

Weeks later, I found myself awake at 4 a.m. and unable to go back to sleep. I looked around for something to read, hoping to relax enough to get back to sleep and my eyes settled on the previously forgotten volume. Again I thought, "Why not?" and I picked it up. I ended up awake much longer because I couldn't put it down.

Bruce introduced a different and possibly quite controversial way of praying. He suggested that we, like Jabez, pray for ourselves first. Many Christians would not agree. They may even consider it a sin to pray for yourself before praying for others. In fact, he suggested we ask GOD for abundant blessings; not just a few.

However, we all know that saying derived from Luke 12:48, which says, "To whom much is given; much is expected." The enlargement of one's territory means new and exciting opportunities. It also means new and more challenging missions.

I began starting every day with the prayer of Jabez. Without a doubt, it worked! God began blessing me with experiences that I never thought would be possible. In fact, there were so many experiences that I became a little overwhelmed. Even more overwhelming were the consequences of those blessings. Family members and people who had been close friends of mine for years began to change. My father, who was my greatest protector, passed away. Suddenly, I discovered that some of the people who I assumed would be my protectors were actually trying to hurt me. They could not be happy about my blessings and jealousy took over. I found myself having to set limits or sever long-term ties with people. It was lonely and frightening. So I decided to stop praying Jabez's prayer because it was too overwhelming.

I continued to pray daily. I just did not pray the Jabez prayer. Things settled down and my territory continued to grow, but at a much more manageable pace. A few years went by, and I grew stronger and wiser.

God began to place different, more positive and encouraging people in my path. Suddenly I realized that most of the people that I spent my time with were actively interested in my success. I also noticed that my gift of discernment helped me to weed potentially toxic people out of my life. It also helped prevent harmful people from entering my life in the first place.

Those realizations brought on a new awareness. It was time for me to go back to praying the prayer of Jabez—this time with a renewed commitment. I made the commitment to make the Jabez prayer a part of my daily prayer ritual. No matter what happened, I would "stand" and keep praying. My borders began to enlarge in ways that I had never considered. My thinking began to change and I found myself consulting God for everything.

I also began doing the things that God told me to do. If he told me to visit a church that I hadn't gone to before, I went. If he told me to call or write someone who I was out of touch with, I did. Whatever I believed God was pushing me to do, I did. The more I did that, the more I discovered new opportunities.

Of course, there were consequences. People seemed to turn against me for no apparent reason.

Other people were around me that I knew I could not trust. I found myself being tried, tested and stretched. Many days, I found myself praying the prayer through tears of frustration, fear and exhaustion, but I kept praying. For a while, I was afraid that nothing that I tried would ever work.

Eventually, I reached what I believed to be a tipping point in my blessings. One of my most passionate prayers was answered. That blessing released a great deal of pressure. It also allowed me to clear my head a little, accept the prayers that had not been answered and figure out my next move. Again, my thinking changed and I began considering doing things that I had never even thought about before.

I still have my share of frustrations and God certainly has not answered all of my prayers. Also, I'm pretty sure that I have more tests and trials to face. As God continues to enlarge my territory, he will continue to stretch and test me. However, it is absolutely clear to me that the blessings that I will enjoy as a result of the prayer are worth every challenge that I will face to receive them.

AN UNLIKELY FRIEND
By Katie Clifton

"When we get together, I want to encourage you in your faith, but I also want to be encouraged by yours" (Romans 1:12, NLT).

"Now faith is being sure of what we hope for and certain of what we do not see" (Hebrews 11:1, NIV)

Six weeks ago, God sent an unlikely new friend into my life. Within hours of meeting her, she had wrecked me and opened my eyes to my sin in such a way that it left me broken, on my knees and weeping. I want to share her story. I don't want to sound boastful or proud, but I want to live out Romans 1:12, so that you may be encouraged in your walk with the Lord.

My new friend's name is Heather. I don't know her last name, I only know that she appeared at our church on a hot Wednesday evening six weeks ago. As I knelt next to her, assessing her needs and listening about the homeless shelter she wanted to be taken to, I was overtaken with the absolute worst smell I have ever encountered. I offered her my sandwich, partly because she looked hungry, and partly because the smell was making me so sick that I couldn't eat my dinner. As we talked outside the church walls, I knew God was telling me not to go inside. This was an opportunity to *be* His church. Little did I know that Heather was about to silently minister to my soul.

It took several minutes of talking with her before I noticed the swarming flies. I tried not to stare at her, and I didn't want to appear to be judging her. The smell, however was repelling me, and something inside me was telling me to walk away. But, God was calling me to act. Heather was menstruating, and as a homeless woman, she was completely ill-equipped for this disastrous situation. Heather needed a shower... and I live 50 yards from the church. My husband and children were all already inside the church, and Heather and I were alone. My mind raced, but I knew God was telling me to trust Him, to respond with love and to take her home with me to offer her a shower, food and clean clothes. God was about to offer me so much more than I had to offer my new friend.

I will spare you the graphic details of how the next hour unfolded, but I am led to share some of the thoughts I had while she was in my home. Never once did I feel fear or worry. God called me to bring her home with me. I had faith that I was being obedient and that the Lord would guide my time with her. I could not see God actively participating (yet) in my interaction with Heather, but I trusted that He would use this time for His glory—this was my hope (Hebrews 11:1). Somewhere in the midst of me trusting the Lord, Satan began speaking to my flesh. I couldn't believe how terrible my nice home smelled. I couldn't really believe that I had brought a woman, filthy and bleeding, into my home. The sights and smells that were in my bathroom caused me to become physically sick—twice. Why did she have to be SO MESSY?! Why did she have to be SO DIRTY?! I had literally just given away a trash bag full of clothes earlier that day, because I was feeling convicted about owning so many clothes and never wearing them. I had given away all that I did not want and kept all that I did. Why was God making me give away some of the things I wanted to hold onto, when I already had been generous?! (Have I mentioned that I am a sinner?) God was revealing ugliness within me and exposing my sin. And He was just getting started.

The shower turned off. Heather was clean. She had all the supplies a woman would need: a clean towel, a box of tampons, clean clothes, underwear, socks, water, toothbrush, deodorant, and food. We got into my car and made the 20 minute drive to the shelter. She called her kids from my phone on the way there. I only heard one side of the conversation, but I heard her say, "Do you know who this is?........Say it again.....Who am I? Please say it again....Who is this....That's right baby, it is MOM." I can't even begin to tell you what this did to my heart. She is a woman in need AND she is a mom. I listened as I could hear her smile while she spoke to her children. I wept.

We arrived, hugged, prayed and I left her at the shelter. Heather was on my heart so heavily that I cried the whole drive back. I walked into my house and knew that I needed to immediately go into my bathroom and begin sterilizing everything. Everywhere I looked had been soiled and the air was still thick with stench. I just kept crying. "Why did she have to be SO FILTHY?! Why did she have to be SO MESSY?!" I filled trash bags with our bath mats, used an entire gallon of bleach and began to use rags instead of paper towels, because the job required extreme cleaning. I began to emotionally break down even more. I had gotten myself in over my head. "Why did I have to bring her into MY house? What had I been thinking?" I was so sick of cleaning up HER MESS. I thought, "JUST LOOK AT ALL THESE FILTHY RAGS!!"

That was it. That was why the Lord brought her into my life. The weight of my own messiness and sin came crashing down on me in a split second. I sat in my bathroom floor sobbing and broken, but this time I was filled with shame. My best is like filthy rags. *"All of us have become like one who is unclean, and all our righteous acts are like filthy rags"* (Isaiah 64:6). I am messy, broken, nasty, unworthy and disgusting. As the weight of my sin and shame became instantly clear I began to say out loud, "Thank you Jesus for her messiness. Thank you Jesus that she was broken and in need. Thank you for sending your Son to pour our His blood, and to still look at my filthy rags and use them for Your glory in spite of myself. Thank you Lord she was messy." I am so thankful that the Lord is faithful. I am so grateful that His love is unending and freely given to anyone who calls on His name. Hebrews Chapter 11 gives accounts and testimonies of men and women of great faith. As I read them all again, I find great strength in their stories of the Lord's faithfulness. Only our Savior takes our brokenness and makes it beautiful. Only He can bring triumph from our tears.

My best may be filthy rags, but we *"know that when your faith is tested, your endurance has a chance to grow. So let it grow, for when your endurance is fully developed, you will be perfect and complete, needing nothing"* (James 1:3-4).

I pray that the Lord will test our faith and find us faithful in all that we do.

RECEIVING REMARKABLE REDEMPTION

Beauty For Ashes Press

LIVING A CHARADE
By Amy Volk

I do as many of you do; I make assumptions about people based on how I perceive them. I make mental assessments as I see the way they look, the things they wear and the cars they drive. The truth is, however, that the outside doesn't always match the inside. I know: acting out a charade is how I spent the better part of my life. I was trying to make up for what I lacked inside, by trying to be perfect on the outside.

I jokingly say that I should be either dead, on drugs or an alcoholic. But it's really no joke. I am simply a product of what happens when Jesus Christ relentlessly pursues and seizes the life of one of His children, and He does what He does best: He makes all things new.

When my parents divorced when I was three, a little, tiny lie planted itself inside my heart: I was not good enough to keep my daddy around. I lived afraid that eventually everyone would leave like he did. The fear of abandonment became a long running theme of my life. I began to understand that to not get hurt, I just needed to self protect. I was not about to let anyone get close to me—or to know the real me.

I was seven when my mom married Fred. Our blended family was pretty awesome at first. Then layoffs and money problems and arguing and pot smoking took over. Even so, my mom kept taking us to the 22nd Street Baptist Church to hear Brother Pollard and it was there that I met Jesus at age 11. One night, just days before my 14th birthday, Fred died. Just like that, we were alone again. But this time, my mom checked out of life as a parent. She just stopped. In her grief and loneliness, she retreated.

Within weeks of his death, I started high school and found a crowd that welcomed me with open arms. This group was the pot smoking, drinking upperclassmen. I felt right at home. For months, I drank, smoked, rode in cars in the desert, fooled around with boys and spent many nights away from home. I also met a 20-year-old man that promised he would take care of me. And he did. And my mom loved him and asked him to move into our house so he could pay rent to her. And he did.

And then...

Then, one day, I missed my period. I was 14 and pregnant.

Alone and terrified, I lied for several weeks about why I was throwing up so much until I finally told my mom. "We'll take care it," she said. That was code for you will have an abortion, and we won't ever talk about it again.

So I had it and we didn't talk about it.

Although I was a Christian, I had no relationship with the Lord, but something in me changed after the abortion. I distanced myself from those friends, that man and I became very academic. I became a cheerleader, I excelled in school and on the outside, I became every parents dream. On the inside, I hated myself. But, the more I performed, the more acceptance I felt. The more success I had, the more I insulated myself from being hurt by anyone. And I believed God hated me too. Guilt, shame and fear drove me. But I had found a way to both hide and be seen all at the same time. I had created my own façade.

I went on to college and graduated. I became a Naval Officer and I moved to Virginia. On my 23rd birthday, just months after leaving my hometown, my mom shot and killed herself. When I heard the news, I had two emotions: absolute devastation and complete relief. Those details are for another time and place, but this time, I wasn't alone in my sorrow. Just 2 months before that event, I had met the man who is now my husband. In His perfect timing, God put Dave in my life. Within six months, we were married. With Dave by my side, I struggled through four years of depression, counseling and endless doubts about God's goodness. Still, in a 10-year span I went on to have two successful careers, gave birth to twins and continued to live with the lie that success equaled acceptance and worth.

At age 30, with twin babies at home, I finally attended my first Bible study. Little did I know that God was beginning to restore my soul, teaching me about His love for me. His graceful hands were molding and holding me. The layers of self-protection began to fall away as He exposed the Enemy's lies in my life. The shame of abortion and my mom's suicide became surrendered to His unfailing Grace. During these important years of learning about Him, He required more of me than I thought I could give—trust, belief, faith and vulnerability. It was hard work to become fully alive and free.

Although I began that grace journey 15 years ago, it's never really over. The gentle hands of Jesus' work continues as He shapes me more and more into His image. What do I still struggle with? Believing in God's goodness toward me, the desire to drink alcohol to the point of drunkenness, selfishness and a long list of other desires of the flesh. But one thing I know: my outside matches my inside now. My tattered heart doesn't need dressing up to be loved or to be accepted to have worth. All my worth is in Him. My worth is because I'm in Christ. My significance is in Him. And what's the one thing that still blows my mind the most? That He *really* likes the *real* me!

Beauty For Ashes Press

MULTIPLE MIRACLES
by Andrea Crowder

Just a few weeks before my 19th birthday, I woke up one afternoon and could hardly pull my head off the pillow. The room was near dark. Even the afternoon sun *trying* to peek through the blinds was fairly unsuccessful.

My mind was in a state of confusion and complete fog. I couldn't hold my head up for long before I passed back out onto the pillow.

When I finally woke up, roughly 25 hours after I had gone to sleep, I wondered how I had survived. That was the last time I did cocaine. Not because I chose to walk away, but because God had a little intervention up His sleeve.

Four weeks later I found out I was pregnant—that pregnancy likely saved my life.

My boyfriend who had just found out that his ex-girlfriend was also pregnant (just two weeks earlier than me) collected me and my things and said goodbye as he dropped me off on the curb at the mall with all of my belongings in a black trash bag and not a penny to my name.

That day was when I hit rock bottom.

Even in the midst of much anxiety and despair, I found hope. I've always had a survivor mentality, and not much could keep me down for long. My beautiful son was growing inside of me, and I knew that we'd have each other. That's all I needed in that moment. My son was my saving grace.

I moved from Seattle to my mom's home in Nevada, got a retail job making $5.75 an hour and took the bus to work each day during my pregnancy to make sure I had money to take care of my son.

This start to my adult life didn't exactly spell a recipe for success. As I look back on this time, I have no idea what God saw in me. Nor do I understand why I'm living the charmed life that I live today—other than because God's love and grace is *so* good!

Although the love of my life had left me during my battle with drugs and alcohol, we reconnected after I moved away. We realized that our hearts for each other had never changed. We were always meant to be, but my addiction drove too deep a wedge between us during the early period of our relationship. About 10 months after we had reconnected, we decided to marry. This year will mark 12 years of marriage for us.

Through all the chaos, I had found love. Our family grew as we welcomed our daughter into the world. I had everything I had every wanted or needed—except one thing.

There was this tug at my heart that just wouldn't go away. You see, my husband—the most beautiful amazing man I've ever met—was a non-believer. All I could keep thinking was that I'd live this brief life with him and I'd spend eternity without my soul mate. It seemed unjust. It wasn't fair.

I'd spend nights laying by his side trying begging him to just come to church with me. I would work to open his mind to a new possibility. I'd cry to him with a broken heart, believing that if he never changed his mind, I'd go to Heaven and he'd go to Hell.

I became resentful towards God. My husband's scientific mind just didn't grasp the concept of God's love or the feeling of the Holy Spirit that I now fully embraced and loved. How could I go to Heaven with all my dirty sin, and he'd go to Hell with all his beauty and goodness? I couldn't—

no I *wouldn't*—accept it. At that moment, I started drifting from my faith. How could a God that was so good allow something so horrible to happen to the love of my life? If that was how He worked, I didn't want anything to do with Him.

And so...I walked away.

Years passed when I felt alone. Looking back I can see that God never left my side. I just wasn't willing to open the door.

Slowly but surely, God started to gently tap on my door, waiting for an invitation back into my life.

I felt this ache...this emptiness...this craving inside of me, just dying to be filled.

I started to look for a new church in the Washington DC area, where the Army had just moved us. It was a slow and hesitant search and after about 12 months, I landed at the doors a community church pastored by a best selling author.

My pastor's humble and authentic approach to teaching really spoke to me, and I started slowing going to church more and more. The vibe and energy of the church made me feel at home. The faith and love of the community really started to feed the craving that I had been feeling.

One day I felt a *strong* prompting to pick up a copy of *The Circle Maker* on my way out of town, even though I was already reading 10 business-related books. I had also promised myself that I wouldn't pick up another book until I had finished some of the books I had started.

I was in a life transition, and I was trying to get my business off the ground so that I could work from home to be more present in my children's lives. I always knew I wanted to be an entrepreneur, and I had finally found my calling. I was hitting speed bump after speed bump, however, as I was trying to build a financial foundation so I could walk away from my corporate job.

As I began to read *The Circle Maker*, it really spoke to me and the struggles I was facing. It teaches you how to pray and lean into God for support in making your biggest dreams come true.

My virtual business includes taking women who have had amazing physical weight loss transformations and teaching them how to run a successful coaching business to pay it forward to others who are still struggling on their journey. I knew that if I could successfully help at least five women grow into strong business leaders, this would translate into enough income for me to walk away from Corporate America.

As I was reading *The Circle Maker* on a flight home from Florida, I began to pray and I asked God, "Please give me five leaders who I can train and serve and bless, and who will equally bless me."

For the first time in my life I heard God speak back. He said, "Five is not enough to glorify my name—15 for you. But you can't go to Italy."

HUH?!

You see, my husband and I had slowly saved enough money over the last 18 months to go on my dream vacation to Italy. A couple of our dearest friends were getting married in Florence and we had agreed to attend and planned to use this opportunity to celebrate our 10-year anniversary.

I honestly thought I was crazy and was hearing things. I thought I had lost my mind to be totally honest with you.

As my plane landed in Washington DC, I decided to send one last prayer up. "God, If I heard you right, you're going to have to tell my husband because he's *never* going to believe me."

Get ready for miracle numero uno.

As I arrived home, I sat down on the couch across from my husband and said, "I have something I need to talk to you about."

With an interested and also concerned look, he gave me his undivided attention.

I explained my prayer and God's response to my request.

Here's the interesting part: My non-believer husband didn't even flinch. His only response was, "Ok. We won't go if you think we should stay."

HUH?!

This was my first lesson on obedience and whoa...it was a big one! Wait till you hear what happened over the next eight months.

So ... we declared that I wasn't going to Italy. Fine, we'll stay home. We figured we'd take that money and put it towards bills.

And here's miracle number two:

I put the book *The Circle Maker* down for about a month. One Saturday night before bed I felt prompted to pick it up and read for a bit. As I'm reading, it talks about giving—sometimes giving beyond your means, even when you have nothing to give.

I felt prompted in my heart that I needed to give more than my normal 10% tithing. So I prayed again. I asked God...*How much? Where?*

Then I went to bed.

The next morning I was crazy busy, (What's new?), and I was considering not going to church. I felt a tug at my heart and decided...nope. I better go. In fact, as I think about it I recall my husband nudging me to get out the door and just go. While he doesn't believe himself, he's very supportive about my beliefs and passions. I truly believe he's more intuitive that he realizes or will ever admit.

On the way to church as the kids chatter in the back seat I began to pray again. "OK God, how much do I need to give? One thousand dollars? I can do that. I'll take it out of the money I saved for Italy."

Then I heard a voice. "All of it."

Come again?

Again...I am certain I'm losing my mind! All of my money? Now I know I said I was willing to get uncomfortable but seriously...*All of it?*

"All of it."

Because we've been actively paying off our debt, we didn't have a huge savings, but we had our money set aside for our Italy trip and also a small extra savings for emergencies.

So I got really real with God and said, "Ok Dude...If you want me to give away *all* of my money, you need to be *really* blunt with me about where that money should go. I'm not going to give it just based off hunch."

(P.S. I think we should all talk to God like a friend. He responds well when I'm being 100% myself while talking to him.)

When I arrived at church that day, we had a guest speaker. He was someone I've never met before. He got up on stage to share what was going on in Africa. Christian persecution is a *huge* problem over there. He shared a story of a young girl who watched her father and brother be shot in the head and killed and was orphaned because they accepted Jesus Christ as their Lord and Savior.

He was trying to find donations of clothing for persecuted Christian families so that they could get to a safe house. They would have leave in the middle of the night with nothing but the clothes on their back.

Then they were also asking for financial donations to help a young girl get her visa to come to the US.

"OK God, I hear you. Loud and clear but *you're* going to have to tell my husband we're doing this, and I think we both know how that's going to go. Good luck."

I called my husband before I left church and told him about hearing God tell me we had to give all our money away. I paused waiting for him to tell me I was nuts. Remember, he's a 100% non-believer.

He didn't.

He said, "Where in Africa? Make sure not to use our debit card, and be careful that it's a secure transaction."

Fine God, you're two for two.

That day we made a donation of $4,321.27 to an orphan fund. It was *all* of our money—savings, checking...*all of it*. Not a single penny left to our names. I walked in faith that God would provide.

Six months later...my business has almost quadrupled, and within 12 months it had grown over 1000%. This explosive growth was miracle three. I was finally able to walk away from my full time corporate job and run my business full time from home.

The kids were on board too. Each of them went to empty their piggy banks to give at Church the next Sunday. Everyone cleaned out their closets to help collect clothes for the families that would flee in the night to seek safety at a shelter.

Months later we received an update at church that the young girl's visa had been denied. They weren't going to let her into the US.

My heart was crushed. I prayed. Hard.

Fast forward a few weeks. My friends were in Italy getting married, and even though I *knew* we'd made the right decision to give the money, I was still sad to miss this special occasion. My heart was hurt to not be there. God knew exactly what I needed to make me feel better.

Again...I almost didn't make it to church this morning. I had so much to do! But a client needed to meet up with me, and that was an easy location for her, so I said I'll just go to church and meet with her after the service.

At the end of service, the gentleman that was working for Tabitha's Orphan's Fund had been making trips back and forth to Africa was there to provide an update. Then our campus pastor also brought a young girl onto the stage.

It was the same girl that couldn't get a visa before.

A family that had *never* been to our church before had showed up on another day that this man had there providing an update. This family had offered to sign an affidavit to help her get her visa. Another family helped her get a scholarship. These were the last two things they needed to reapply for her visa.

Getting this girl a visa was miracle #4.

I lost it.

I began bawling right there in my seat. God knew I had to be at church that Sunday to see this miracle standing before me. That's why he told me I couldn't go to Italy. Otherwise I would have landed in Italy that Sunday morning. I would have never met this beautiful miracle child, who was wearing a princess dress.

I walked up to her after church and congratulated her. I told the gentleman that I was putting their information on my website to help raise money for the orphan fund, and asked if I could take a photo with them.

Neither of them knew who I was, nor did they know that it was our family that donated the money. That's fine—I didn't care—but I needed that photo for me. To remind me that even when we can't see God's entire plan, and even when he asks us to do things that make *no* sense, we have to walk in faith and know that he has a bigger vision for our lives.

I still can't tell this entire story without tearing up. I'm so deeply honored that God trusted me enough to put this in my hands.

I will never forget that year of my life. God speaks. He is loud and clear if you stop long enough to listen. Trust him. He's got *big* plans for you life.

Although my husband is still a non-believer, I do believe God is working slowly into his heart. I'll continue to radiate God's love and offer my life in service of His plan. Just because I can't see God's progress in his heart, doesn't mean it's not there. I'll leave that between God and my husband.

ABOUT THE AUTHORS

Linda Bingham is first and foremost a blood bought, born again, child of the King, a wife to her best friend, a mom to beautiful children -a son and daughter from birth and two beautiful daughters from "I do", a Gigi to 4 precious little ones and counting.

The past 25 years Linda has spent in various businesses, each one building upon the other to allow her to be who God has purposed for today. Currently it is Linda's mission to share experiences, knowledge and know-how with others so you can be encouraged, grow, and be blessed beyond measure in your health, business and everyday life.

Linda is preparing to release her first book, *I Woke Up Fat, I Woke Up Skinny* focusing on the power of our everyday thoughts that keep us imprisoned to living a unhealthy lifestyle. She is also writing a second book titled *The 30 Day Life*, focusing on creating the life you are intended to live 30 days at a time through better health, business practices, and everyday living.

Connect with Linda at **Twitter.com/LindaBingham** and **Facebook.com/lindabinghambusinesscoach**

Esly Regina Carvalho, Ph.D. maintained a private practice in the Dallas area for many years before her return to Brazil in 2006. A Brazilian-American clinical psychologist, she now directs the TraumaClinic in Brasilia, and spends extended time training EMDR professionals.

An international trainer and speaker in great demand, Esly has also published books and articles about the use of EMDR and Psychodrama (her first training approach). She founded the Psychodrama movement in Ecuador in 1990, which now boasts several training groups. She brought EMDR therapy to Brazil as well, where over fifteen hundred therapists have been trained in this modality, and has been instrumental in the national development of EMDR.

She directs a small Christian ministry in Brazil called Praça do Encontro, dedicated to helping people overcome the challenges of life.

Esly is married and enjoys spending with her family, *especially those grandchildren!*

Katie Clifton is a church planting pastor's wife, mother of 4, speaker, writer, blogger at **Mireandmanna.com**, lover of adoption and advocate for missions.

She loves good food, coffee and especially loves Jesus.

Her heart is in Kenya, her home is in Arkansas.

In February 2015 Jared (Katie's husband) and a handful of **faithful (read: crazy) friends launched a church (www.renewchurchar.com) with the desire to simply preach the gospel, love people like Christ taught and live intentionally on mission for the glory of God.

Their desire is for the church to be a bridge for racial unity within their community, a place for the broken to feel welcome and for all to come and experience an authentic relationship with Jesus Christ.

Katie serves as the Missions Advocate for African Christian Outreach (ACO). ACO is a grass roots East African ministry focusing on equipping, engaging and empowering people through relationships, service, Bible study, community investment, orphan care, discipleship and evangelism.

You can partner with Katie in ministry and serve in East Africa with her by visiting **Acokenya.org.** To have Katie Clifton speak at your church or event please contact her at **katieclifton00@gmail.com.**

Elin Criswell is a Jesus follower, wife, mom, soapmaker and author who gains great encouragement simply by encouraging others. She lives in Central Texas with her husband, Danny and family. Elin's blog is **TheCountrySoaper.com.** Her books include *Bubbles to Bucks: How to Make Money Selling Soap* and *Creative Soap Making.*

Andrea Crowder helps women create physical and financial wealth, freedom and joy, unapologetically, so they can show up in the world in a bigger and more audacious way. Whether it's a fit and fabulous bod, or a financial freedom (or both!) Andrea is the coach who will help you drop 'average' and start living the life you were meant to live. Connect with Andrea at her website, **AndreaCrowderFitness.com** or **Facebook.com/AndreaCrowderFitness.**

Kayla Fioravanti is a wife, mother, author and speaker. Kayla is happily married to her serial entrepreneur husband Dennis. They are the blessed parents of Keegan, Selah and Caiden. Kayla and her family live in Franklin, Tennessee. Kayla is the Managing Editor of *360 Degrees of Grief*. Kayla's blogs are **KaylaFioravanti.com**, **Selah-Press.com** and **GogoNaughtyPaws.com**. Books by Kayla include: *How to Self-Publish: The Author-preneur's Guide to Publishing*; *How to Make Melt & Pour Soap Base from Scratch*; *The Art, Science & Business of Aromatherapy*; *DIY Kitchen Chemistry* and poetry *When I was Young I Flew the Sun Like a Kite*.

Julene Fleurmond has a deep passion for inspiring others to overcome the pain in their past to rediscover their deepest dreams and boldly pursue their purpose. After living many years in fear, social anxiety and shame she has found her voice and is sharing the truth and power of God's deep love as an author, visual artist, inspirational speaker and singer.

As the founder and editor of the online faith-based publication **DreaminSoul.com,** Julene inspires you to live your God-given dreams on purpose to spread the love of Christ wherever He's placed you. She also designs the inspirational clothing and gift line at **Envibrance.com** that spreads encouragement while raising funds to help various causes.

As an artist, Julene loves to serve others' dreams through graphic design services, as she has done for more than 10 years. In her upcoming book *Live On Purpose* she shares the seeds of wisdom God planted in her heart on living an extraordinary life full of meaning and embracing the greatness within you.

Julene is a free-spirited dreamer and big kid at heart. She loves everything colorful, sparkly and Disney (one of her crazy big dreams is to star in a Disney movie some day – why not dream big, with God anything is possible!) Her organization The Dare Dreamer Movement inspires people to live their deepest dreams creatively and reconnect with their childhood to see the world with wonder and awe.

Connect with Julene at **DreamFleur.com, Twitter.com/dreamfleur, Facebook.com/julenedreamfleur** and **Instagram.com/dreamfleur** .

Dr. Lori M. Hobson (Dr. Lori) received her Bachelor's Degree in Psychology from Norfolk State University. Her Master's degree in Rehabilitation Counseling came from Hunter College in NYC. Her Doctorate in Organizational Leadership is from Nova Southeastern University in Florida.

Dr. Lori is one of very few experts researching and writing on the subject of resilience in women leaders. She is a certified life coach and a member of the faculty at South University, Virginia Beach. She is also an accomplished motivational speaker and trainer. She has developed and presented workshops for a number of local, state, and national organizations. She was also a finalist and founding case study author in the "Hot Mommas Project" competition through George Washington University's School of Entrepreneurship and Dr. Lori is a professional member of the National Speakers Association.

Dr. Lori's book, *Momma Sayings and Life Reflections*, puts a twist on *Life's Little Instruction Book*. Lori takes everyday witticisms shared by her family members (and those of others) and combines them to entertain and educate. She uses her expertise as a counselor, life coach, and trainer to teach valuable life lessons. Her witty and genuine style of storytelling takes you from laughter to tears and back again.
Set Yourself Free: A 30-Day Planner for Improving Your Most Important Life Areas is more than just a 30-day planner, it is designed to be a tool for developing a strategy for your life. It is a great introduction to life coaching.

Dr. Lori's website is **LoriHobson.com** and her email is **DrLori@resiliensintl.com.**

Vanessa Hlavaty was born and raised in Buffalo, NY. Now living in Louisville, KY she spends time enjoying life with a wonderful husband of 23 years, their 4 year old son, and their 7 year old fur child: a border collie named Cecil. Vanessa owns her own online boutique, **TheBraidedBoutique.com** and also works for a handcrafted bath & body company. An aspiring author, Vanessa has several projects that will be published in 2016.

Mary Humphrey is a Christian author and life coach. She can be found at **Wisewomanofnoblecharacter.com**. She has four books published and several others currently being written via His Pasture Press. Mary's mission is to help women realize their God-given talents and to follow their resulting passions, through an encouragement to grow an in-depth relationship with Christ, with her motto being Share, Encourage and Grow. Mary maintains blogs at **Anniesgoathill.com, Hispasturepress.com,** and **Maryhumphreycoaching.com.** Mary's books include *Advanced Soap Making: Removing the Mystery, Essential Soapmaking, Essential Lotion Making: Skin Care Made Easy,* and *Annie's all about Goats: Essential Goat Care.*

Beverly Dru Lewis is an Executive Trainer, Speaker and Business Coach. She is the CEO (Chief Encouragement Officer) of **BeverlySpeaks.com** and author of *Win From Within: The Heart of Success and Significance.* Her first book is born out of 35 years of work with over 10,000 professionals, in-depth research on leadership, communication and lessons from her entrepreneurial ventures. Beverly lives in Florida with her husband of 36 years. They have three grown children and four grandchildren.

Connect with Beverly at **Twitter.com/Beverly Speaks, Facebook.com/BeverlyLewisSpeaks** and **Linkedin.com/BeverlyDruLewis**. Her email is **Beverly@BeverlySpeaks.com.**

Alyssa Middleton is a wife, mother, entrepreneur and author passionate about helping others achieve their dreams. She owns **AJMurrays.com**, a men's grooming products company and **BathandBodyAcademy.com**, where she teaches and coaches other beauty business owners how to grow their companies and reach their goals. Alyssa is also the Managing Editor of Beauty From Ashes Press and loves touching the lives of others through the written word. She lives in Louisville, KY with her family and hyperactive rescue dog. Alyssa's books include *Essential Soap Making, Advanced Soapmaking: Removing the Mystery, Introduction to Artisan Perfumery* and the Kindle book series, *Beauty Business Basics*. She is currently working on her first novel.

Cheryl Moses is a mother of two, entrepreneur, coach, and author who uses her savvy style to help success driven moms and women of all walks of life, achieve their goals and pursue their dreams of having a freedom lifestyle. As a woman of God, Cheryl uses her spiritual point of view to get her message across and mentor those in need of knowing their worth and their purpose in life. Cheryl is the founder of New Eminence, a consulting firm that specializes in equipping single moms to use their God inspired gifts to build successful brands and businesses on the web. She also has a web design business called New Eminence Designs to provide custom graphics, content, and marketing materials for business owners. Cheryl is a co-author in *Head Ladies in Charge*, and has written *Small Changes, Big Manifestation,*

Girl Talk Self Talk Real Talk, and *Beyond the Break Room,* all available on Amazon Kindle.

Cheryl's website is **Cheryljmoses.com** and you can connect with her at **Facebook.com/CheryljMoses** and **Twitter.com/innovatherlife**

Loral Robben Pepoon has enjoyed spending the last two years working as a freelance editor, writer, marketer and project manager. For more than 15 years, Loral served as a managing editor, creative director and marketing manager at major corporations and non-profits in downtown Chicago. Loral followed her love of God's creation and exchanged seeing the impressive architecture of downtown Chicago daily to live in the natural beauty and warmer climate in Tennessee. She holds a Master of Journalism/Advertising from the University of Kansas and a Bachelor of Arts in European Studies/ French and German from the University of Tulsa. In her free time, she enjoys spending time with her amazing husband, dance fitness, cooking, hiking, reading, cooking, paddle boarding, kayaking and traveling.

Loral's website is **Cowriterpro.com**. Connect with her at **Linkedin.com/in/loralrobbenpepoon** and **Facebook.com/LoralRobbenPepoon**.

Patricia "Pat" Sabiston is a sought-after trainer, motivator, and writing instructor. She has published books, essays, short stories, articles, fillers, and interviews. Her work has appeared in the *Atlanta Journal/Constitution, New York Times/Asbury Park Press Edition, NPR Online,* and *The Southern Poetry Review* among other outlets.

As owner of THE WRITE PLACE, a communications consulting firm, Pat's daily routine is writing – advertising copy; radio, TV, and video scripts; newsletters, brochures, press releases and grants, speeches and training curriculum.

Pat is originally from North Carolina where it is said that if you throw a rock-"nine out of ten times you'll hit a writer". She has made Panama City, Florida her home since 1992.

Pat LOVES Her Lord and Savior, Jesus Christ, her best friend, Tom Sabiston, their children, grandchildren, and precious GREAT Granddaughter, their Miniature Schnauzer, Harley, and Crème Brulee. Connect with Pat at **PatSabistonAuthor.com, Facebook.com/PatSabistonAuthor, Linkedin.com/in/pat-sabiston-89b43964** and **patsabiston@irawriter.com.**

Susan Sexton resides in a small Kentucky town with her husband and two children. She is a substitute teacher and is active in her church's children's ministry. She enjoys camping and traveling with her family. Her hope has always been to share her story of loss and is thankful for the opportunity to do so.

 **Cindy Taylor** is wife to an amazing husband and mom to 4 awesome children (and an equally awesome son-in-law) and an amazingly awesome grandson! For the past 20 years, she invested time homeschooling her children and running a successful Direct Sales business. As 3 of her children graduated, the youngest studying independently and her business winding down, Cindy became a woman without a mission! After some soul searching and studying, Cindy became a Certified Coach. She now works with women who are without a mission and on the journey to "What's Next?" Connect with Cindy at **Facebook.com/cindybizcareerstrategies** or learn more about her at **Cindybiz.com**.

 **Alicia Terry** is a communications professional, trainer/facilitator, and public speaker. She is also the soon to be author of the book, *I Am Who God Says I Am*. Through her blossoming business ministry she helps women, entrepreneurs, and teens live and leave legacies that fully allows them to demonstrate the glory of God. Connect with Alicia at **AliciaTerry.com**, **Twitter.com/yesiamalicia** and **Facebook.com/yesiamalicia**.

Amy Volk is a writer, blogger, organizer, and former Registered Nurse. But mostly she is a mom to Mallory and Riley and wife to Dave. These days you can find her writing on her blogs, AmyVolk.com and CaveMamas.com, cooking up Paleo recipes and trying her best to lift heavy weights in CrossFit.

She has a no-so-secret obsession with shoes and is currently writing her first book, *Coffee, Shoes, and Jesus*. Because shoes, of course. And Jesus.

Jennifer Waddle is best known for words of encouragement as an author, speaker and musician for Women's Ministry. She currently has three published books on Amazon and is a regular contributor for **WomensMinistryTools.com** and **GotQuestions.org**.

In her Speaking Ministry, *Encouraging Women Everywhere, in Faith...in Life,* Jennifer is committed to sharing authentic messages of hope to women of all walks of life. She loves being a wife of 24 years, mom of four, and nana of two. Most of all, she cherishes her time spent in the Word of God, with a cup of coffee and a beautiful view of the Rocky Mountains.

Contact Jennifer at **www.jenniferwaddleonline.com** or **encouragementmama@gmail.com**

ACKNOWLEDGMENTS

First, I'd like to acknowledge the author/speaker who gave me the courage to share my story of transformation after hearing her speak so candidly of hers. I never would have imagined her story would mirror portions of my own. Thank you, L., for your candor and willingness to share the darker parts of your past to further illuminate Christ's love and redeeming power.

Thanks be to God for the consistent nudges to create a compilation book and for allowing my paths to cross with so many strong, transformed and redeemed sisters in Christ.

To my fellow contributors: thank you for your transparency and for contributing your powerful stories. I know the stories within these pages will bless the lives of those who read them and it is my prayer that by seeing the transformations that took and continue to take place in our lives, that they'll humbly submit to His Lordship.

Thank you to Jennifer for the beautiful cover design that so aptly represents these stories. Thank you to Loral, my editor for coming up with the section titles and for making the style consistent among the various contributors.

Finally, to all readers, thank you for taking the time to read our personal stories. I pray this book and the stories within have touched and encouraged you. I pray that whenever any of us face trials and tribulations, that we would humble ourselves and allow the love and sacrifice of Christ Jesus to wipe away our tears and transform our lives.

www.ingramcontent.com/pod-product-compliance
Lightning Source LLC
Chambersburg PA
CBHW061323040426
42444CB00011B/2747